DOUBLE INDEMNITY

5/1/09

For Kelsey —
in remembrance of noir
+ your fabulous work.
you should be proud!
"straight down the line,
baby — straight
down the line."

All my best —

Mark

**SCREENPLAYS
BY BILLY WILDER**

Double Indemnity

The Lost Weekend

Stalag 17

Sunset Boulevard

DOUBLE INDEMNITY

BILLY WILDER

screenplay by
BILLY WILDER
RAYMOND CHANDLER

with an introduction by
JEFFREY MEYERS

UNIVERSITY OF CALIFORNIA PRESS
BERKELEY / LOS ANGELES / LONDON

University of California Press
Berkeley and Los Angeles, California

University of California Press, Ltd.
London, England

Published by permission of Billy Wilder,
© 2000 by The Regents of the University of California.

The screenplay reproduced here is a facsimile of the original
shooting script. Some digital manipulation was performed
in order to improve type quality.

Library of Congress Cataloging-in-Publication Data

Wilder, Billy, 1906–

Double indemnity / Billy Wilder ; screenplay by Billy
Wilder, Raymond Chandler ; with an introduction by
Jeffrey Meyers.

p.   cm.

ISBN 978-0-520-21848-2 (pbk. : alk. paper)

I. Chandler, Raymond, 1888–1959. II. Meyers, Jeffrey.
III. Double indemnity (Motion picture). IV. Title.

PN1997.D6553 W55 2000
791.43′72—dc21

00-025044
CIP

Printed in the United States of America

08 07 06

10 9 8 7 6 5 4

The paper used in this publication is both acid-free and
totally chlorine-free (TCF). The paper used in this publication
meets the minimum requirements of ANSI/NISO Z39.48-1992
(R 1997) (*Permanence of Paper*).

INTRODUCTION TO DOUBLE INDEMNITY

JEFFREY MEYERS

I

DOUBLE INDEMNITY, a classic *film noir*, concerns sex, greed and loathing, murder, conscience and guilt. The novel that inspired the movie was considered impossible to film. The Hollywood censorship office had rejected the brutal story, characterizing it as a blueprint for murder that allows the adulterous lovers to cheat the law and ends with a double suicide. Its director and coauthor of the script, Billy Wilder, found a way to finesse these objections by writing the screenplay in the form of a confession and closing the film with the murderers' retribution and death.

Wilder, who inspired great performances from previously undistinguished actors Fred MacMurray and Barbara Stanwyck, reached Hollywood by a circuitous route. He was born in 1906 in Sucha (thirty miles south of Kraców) in Polish Galicia, then part of the Austro-Hungarian Empire. As a child he witnessed the collapse of the decadent empire after World War I and acquired a sardonic view of the frailty of personal relations. The son of a hotelier and smalltime businessman, he briefly studied law at the University of Vienna, then became a newspaper reporter there and in Berlin, where he supplemented his income by working as a dance partner and gigolo. With Robert Siodmak and Fred Zinnemann, he made the German documentary film *People on Sunday* (1929), and when Hitler came to power in 1933, he fled to Paris. There, he directed his first feature film, *Mauvaise Graine* (Bad Seed), with Danielle Darrieux. In 1934 he reached Hollywood, where he roomed with his fellow exile Peter Lorre.

In 1943 Wilder adapted and directed James M. Cain's novel *Double Indemnity* (1936) for the screen. The book was inspired by the Ruth Snyder–Judd Gray case of 1927, in which a New York woman and her lover were convicted of murdering her husband with a window sash. In "Echoes of the Jazz Age," Scott Fitzgerald noted that the newspapers had sensationalized the horrific details of her execution: "in prison Ruth Snyder had to be hoisted into [the Jazz Age] by the tabloids—she was, as *The Daily News* hinted deliciously to gourmets, about 'to cook, *and sizzle*, AND FRY!' in the electric chair."[1] Edmund Wilson added that Cain was "particularly ingenious in tracing from their first beginnings the tangles that gradually tighten around the necks of people involved in these bizarre and brutal crimes that figure in the American papers."[2] In the film Wilder streamlined the story of the murderers' gradual entrapment.

"Double indemnity" is a clause in a life insurance policy that pays twice the face value in the event of accidental death. In both novel and film the wife and the insurance agent trick the husband into taking out a policy on his own life and plan to murder him to collect the money. In Cain's novel Huff (called Neff in the film) tells the story and emphasizes—in tough-guy style—the difference between appearance and reality: "He knows all about this policy, and yet he don't know a thing about it. He applies for it, in writing, and yet he don't apply for it. He pays me for it with his own check, and yet he don't pay me. He has an accident happen to him, and yet he don't have an accident happen to him. He gets on the train, and yet he don't get on it."

In the novel, despite some clever business with the victim's cigar, the murder is typically graphic and gruesome: "I raised up, put my hand over his mouth, and pulled his head back. He grabbed my hand in both of his. The cigar was still in his fingers. I took it with my free hand and handed it to her. She took it. I took one of the crutches and hooked it under his chin. I won't tell you what I did then. But in two seconds he was curled down on the seat with a broken neck." In the film the murder is portrayed more obliquely and dramatically. The camera focuses on Phyllis Dietrichson (Barbara Stanwyck) as Walter Neff (Fred MacMurray) kills her husband. Her icy expression, with its hint of satisfaction, registers the murder and conveys her ruthless personality.

In both novel and film, Huff/Neff, realizing that he has been manipulated and trapped by a treacherous woman, admits: "I had killed a man, for money and a woman. I didn't have the money and I didn't have the woman. The woman was a killer, out-and-out, and she had made a fool of me. She had used me for a cat's paw so she could have another man, and she had enough on me to hang me higher than a kite."[3] The ending of the novel is weak—even absurd. The insurance company, not wanting the public to know that their agent is a murderer, forces Huff to write out a confession and puts him on a boat to Mexico—with Phyllis. She convinces him to commit suicide, and the book ends as they prepare to jump into the sea. Wilder's very different conclusion is much more effective.

Wilder followed the novel's basic plot, but invented most of the film's distinctive elements: Neff's voice-over confession, the flashback to his involvement with Phyllis, and his intense bond with his older colleague, the claims investigator Barton Keyes (Edward G. Robinson). He put some witty double entendres in Neff and Phyllis's dialogue, and used the simple device of a stalled car to increase the tension. MacMurray praised Wilder's superb sense of timing in that scene: "Barbara and I sat in this dummy car. Just a car seat. No dashboard. No ignition key to turn. We faked it, pantomimed it. When I changed places with her and turned the key I remember I was doing it fast and Billy kept saying, '*Make it longer, make it longer*,' and finally I yelled, '*For Chrissake Billy, it's not going to hold that long*,' and he said, '*Make it longer*,' and he was right. It held."[4] Cain, greatly impressed by the film, said: "Billy Wilder did a terrific job. It's the only picture I ever saw made from my books that had things in it I wish I had thought of. Wilder's ending was much better than my ending, and his device for letting the guy tell the story by taking out the office dictating machine—I would have done it if I had thought of it."[5]

Though Wilder always wrote with a coauthor, his usual collaborator, the urbane Charles Brackett, thought the novel grisly and disgusting, and refused to work on the project. Cain was writing another filmscript and was unavailable. Raymond Chandler, who considered himself infinitely superior to Cain, also found the book repulsive: "James Cain—faugh! Everything he touches smells like a billygoat. He is every kind of writer I detest, a faux naif, a Proust in greasy overalls. . . . Such people are the offal of literature, not because they write about dirty things, but because they do it in a dirty way."[6] But Chandler agreed to collaborate for the money (he naively asked for only $1,000 and got about $10,000; Wilder earned $44,000) and for the experience of working with Wilder.

Both writers, temperamentally mismatched, immediately disliked each other and remained hostile throughout their three months' work on the script. Chandler found the anger and tension depressing; Wilder found them stimulating. He later described his disillusionment on first meeting Chandler, a former alcoholic who was then fifty-five years old: "I was very surprised. I had imagined, after reading *The Big Sleep*, a kind of Philip Marlowe. I envisioned a former private detective, like Dashiell Hammett, who had worked his own experiences into literature. But he was an awkward, pale, elderly man, who made a somewhat strange impression. He wore a frayed, checkered tweed jacket, with leather patches on the elbows, and gray, worn-out flannel trousers. He had a sickly complexion, like a man who's drowned himself in drink."[7]

Since Chandler didn't know how to write a screenplay, Wilder gave him a copy of the novel and his own script *Hold Back the Dawn* (1941) as a model and told Chandler to do some work over the weekend. On Monday, Chandler turned up with eighty pages, which Wilder thought were quite useless: "He had that idiotic idea that if you know about 'fade in' and 'dissolve' and 'closeup,' and 'the camera moves into the keyhole' and so on, that you have mastered the art of writing pictures. He had no idea how these things were done."[8]

Wilder was volatile, Chandler phlegmatic, and their work habits were comically antithetical. Wilder's biographer explains:

He seldom sat still, but would pace back and forth like a restless animal, brandishing a malacca cane, which sometimes swung uncomfortably close to Chandler's head. He wore his hat indoors, which Chandler regarded as the height of rudeness. Even more uncivil was his habit of retreating to the bathroom more often than a normal bladder required—Wilder traditionally went there to have a smoke or stimulate his thinking process, but more and more it was to retreat from his fussy collaborator.

"He did not like me very much," Wilder admits. "He was in Alcoholics Anonymous, and I think he had a tough time with me—I drove him back into drinking. Also he didn't like it because I was a bachelor then [in fact, Wilder was married] and I had all the pretty girls at Paramount and he had nothing. So he complained that I wasn't serious about the script—I was very serious about the script! But I did not dedicate my entire life to writing scripts—I also had a private life."[9]

Chandler, standing on his English sense of dignity and decorum, formally complained to the Paramount executives and demanded a radical change in Wilder's behavior: "Mr. Wilder was at no time to swish under Mr. Chandler's nose or to point in his direction the thin, leather-handled malacca cane which Mr. Wilder was in the habit of waving around while they worked. Mr. Wilder was not to give Mr. Chandler orders of an arbitrary or personal nature such as 'Ray, will you open the window?' or 'Ray, will you shut that door, please.'"[10] Years later, when asked about the best film he'd ever worked on, Chandler eliminated Wilder's role in the scriptwriting and took sole credit: "Without question, *Double Indemnity*, which I wrote for an odd little director with a touch of genius, Billy Wilder."[11] He also admitted that working with Wilder "was an agonizing experience and had probably shortened my life, but I learned from it as much about screenwriting as I am capable of learning, which is not very much."[12]

II

We know at the start of the film that Neff is the murderer, and we immediately want to know how he became a killer and how he was caught. As in Poe's "Purloined Letter," Keyes, the claims investigator, doesn't see what "was smack up against [his] nose." Wilder chose to begin the film with Neff's late-night confession into a dictating machine so that, he said, "we can concentrate on what follows—their efforts to escape, the net closing, closing" in the beautifully constructed script.[13] Neff first meets Phyllis when he stops by her house to renew her husband's automobile insurance and notices the connection between her "Spanish craperoo"–style house and her sleazy character. Instead of the usual squeaky-clean setting, Wilder explained, "I'd go in and kind of dirty up the sets a little bit and make them look worn. I'd take the white out of everything. . . . I wanted that look that Californian houses get, with the sun streaming through the shutters and showing the dust. You couldn't photograph that, so [the cameraman, John] Seitz made some shreddings for me and they photographed like motes in sunbeams. I like that kind of realism."[14]

In this context, Phyllis's femme fatale entrance is stunning. Looking down at Neff from a staircase landing, she wears only a bath towel, pom-pommed slippers, and a gold ankle bracelet. Her deliberately cheap-looking platinum-blonde wig provoked one producer to complain: "We hire Barbara Stanwyck and here we get George Washington."[15] Neff, who has smelled the honeysuckle on the way in, is enchanted by her perfume and chained by her anklet. Sensing her availability, he mentions that her insurance, like her body, is "not fully covered." When she says she has just been sunbathing, he imagines her naked and makes the cynically flirtatious remark: "No pigeons around, I hope."

Neff's ironic mixture of insurance pitch and seductive come-on leads directly to the brilliant dialogue, with its threats of punishment and tears, in which each tries to top the other with the next cheeky supposition:

PHYLLIS: There's a speed limit in this state, Mr. Neff. Forty-five miles an hour.
NEFF: How fast was I going, officer?
PHYLLIS: I'd say about ninety.
NEFF: Suppose you get down off your motorcycle and give me a ticket.
PHYLLIS: Suppose I let you off with a warning this time.
NEFF: Suppose it doesn't take.
PHYLLIS: Suppose I have to whack you over the knuckles.
NEFF: Suppose I bust out crying and put my head on your shoulder.
PHYLLIS: Suppose you try putting it on my husband's shoulder.
NEFF: That tears it.

The driving metaphor takes on greater significance when they murder Dietrichson in his car and then have trouble starting it as they try to escape. In a similar way, the recurrent expression "straight down the line" suggests both the railroad tracks where they drag Dietrichson's body (Neff runs off with his fake cast shining in the dark) and a one-way trip to the cemetery at "the end of the line." Neff knows that Phyllis is trying to entrap him and that it will be almost impossible to deceive Keyes, who has been called in to investigate the claim. But—both sexually attracted and morally repelled—he proceeds to his doom with open eyes.

Neff's relationship with his father figure and father-confessor, Barton Keyes, who tries to recruit his protégé to the more intellectual claims department, is enhanced by Wilder's casting against type. He gave Mac-Murray, sometime saxophonist and star of genial comedies, the murderer's role and turned Robinson—who'd built his reputation as the gangster in *Little Caesar* (1930) and who would soon revert to a criminal role as Johnny Rocco in *Key Largo* (1948)—into the intuitive Holmesian investigator. Keyes's character is suggested by his conservative vest, watch chain, pens, and cigars, and by his deep distrust of women. He calls Neff "Walter," though Neff deferentially calls him "Keyes"; and Neff suggests his close connection with Keyes by supplying the matches that his friend always seems to lose. The real love story is not between Neff and Phyllis, but between Neff and Keyes. Neff's criminal betrayal of his friend and mentor gives the tawdry story a new dimension.

The only weakness in the film is the poorly acted subplot with Phyllis's stepdaughter, Lola, and Lola's boyfriend, Nino. Neff befriends Lola, who hates Phyllis. The younger woman tells him that Phyllis had attempted to kill Lola's mother and later tried on a widow's black hat while her husband was still alive. Toward the end, when the two couples seem to have shifted allegiance—Neff shows fatherly concern for Lola, and Phyllis has become obsessed with the handsome young Nino—Neff tells Nino that Lola still loves him and encourages him to go back to her.

At first, the murder appears to succeed when Neff, in a fake cast, impersonates Dietrichson and falls off the slow-moving train, and when Neff and Phyllis barely manage to escape some close calls. Just as Keyes nearly runs into Phyllis (hiding behind a door) when he unexpectedly turns up at Neff's apartment, so Jackson (who saw Neff just before he jumped off the train) nearly identifies Neff in Keyes's office. But the murderers, filled with distrust, soon turn against each other. They have changed greatly since their first meeting and are now more afraid of each other than of Keyes, who is on their trail. During Neff's voice-over confession, he suddenly says: "I couldn't hear my own footsteps. It was the walk of a dead man."

As in a Western movie, Neff and Phyllis both bring guns for the final shoot-out. The radio plays "Tangerine," a haunting pop song whose lyrics express disillusionment about an egoistic woman: "Yes, she has them all on the run / But her heart belongs to just one—Tangerine." In a reversal of their first seductive scene, Phyllis admits: "We're both rotten, Walter," and he bitterly replies: "Only you're just a little more rotten. You're rotten clear through." She wounds him, and just before he kills her, she confesses that she never loved him or anyone else.

Phyllis, completely evil and cold blooded, has destroyed a once-decent man. Neff is much more complex and ambiguous. Though he has killed both Dietrichson and Phyllis, his redeeming features make him a sympathetic character. He's gently paternal with Lola, and he has a strong friendship with Keyes. He really loved Phyllis—and killed to get her. He feels remorse and is compelled to confess his crimes. Though bleeding to death in the office, he continues to wisecrack till the very end. When Keyes, summoned by the janitor, turns up in person in the middle of the night while Neff is dictating a message to him, Neff remarks: "I always wondered what time you got down to work." And when Neff can't get down the corridor, let alone escape to Mexico, he says: "somebody moved the elevator a couple of miles away." (There's one logical flaw: if he wanted to escape across the border—Phyllis's aphrodisiac perfume came from Ensenada—why didn't he go straight to Mexico and confess there instead of going to Keyes's office?)

This screenplay contains an alternate ending, sequence "E," now published for the first time, in which Keyes watches Neff's execution in the gas chamber. Wilder built an expensive set—said to cost $150,000 but actually budgeted at $4,700—and recorded all the morbidly realistic details: "In *Double Indemnity*," he said, "I had a final scene with the character in the gas chamber. There are pellets dropping and the bucket and the fumes, and outside is Eddie Robinson watching. They are two great friends, and there is something going on between them, an exchange or whatever. It was very good but just unnecessary. The picture is over when [Keyes] tells [Neff], 'You'll never even make the elevator,' and he tries and collapses. In the distance you hear the siren of the police, and you know what's going to happen."[16] Though Wilder called this scene one of the best he'd ever shot (it disappeared into the Paramount vaults and has never been screened), he realized that it was too gruesome, heavy-handed and self-righteous, both anticlimactic and superfluous. This omission strengthens the script.

Double Indemnity was nominated for seven Academy Awards: for best picture, director, and screenplay, as well as for best actress, cinematography, score, and sound. But it lost out completely to the heart-warming and sentimental *Going My Way*, with Bing Crosby as a Catholic priest, and didn't win any Academy Awards. *Going My Way* has been forgotten, while *Double Indemnity*, as Woody Allen observed, "has all the characteristics of the classic forties film. . . . It's in black and white, it has fast badinage, it's very witty, a story from the great age. It has . . . the tough voice-over. It has brilliantly written dialogue, and the perfect score by Miklos Rozsa. It's Billy Wilder's best movie—but practically anyone's best movie."[17]

NOTES

1. F. Scott Fitzgerald, "Echoes of the Jazz Age," in *The Crack-Up*, ed. Edmund Wilson (New York: New Directions, 1945), p. 18.

2. Edmund Wilson, "The Boys in the Back Room: James M. Cain," in *Classics and Commercials* (1950; New York: Vintage, 1962), p. 21.

3. James M. Cain, *Double Indemnity*, in *Three of a Kind* (New York: Knopf, 1943), pp. 236–237, 259–260, 294.

4. Maurice Zolotow, *Billy Wilder in Hollywood* (New York: Putnam, 1977), p. 16.

5. Quoted in Pat McGilligan, ed., *Backstory: Interviews with Screenwriters of Hollywood's Golden Age* (Berkeley: University of California Press, 1986), p. 125.

6. Raymond Chandler, *Selected Letters*, ed. Frank MacShane (New York: Columbia University Press, 1981), p. 23.

7. Hellmuth Karasek, *Billy Wilder: Eine Nahaufnahme* (A Close-Up) (Hamburg: Hoffmann und Campe, 1992), p. 259.

8. Kevin Lally, *Wilder Times: The Life of Billy Wilder* (New York: Henry Holt, 1996), pp. 128–129.

9. Lally, *Wilder Times*, p. 129.

10. Frank MacShane, *The Life of Raymond Chandler* (1976; New York: Penguin, 1978), p. 109.

11. Quoted in Peter Forster, "Gentle Tough Guy," *John O'London's Weekly* 62 (March 6, 1953), p. 189.

12. Chandler, *Selected Letters*, p. 237.

13. MacShane, *Life of Raymond Chandler*, p. 108.

14. Charles Higham and Joel Greenberg, *The Celluloid Muse: Hollywood Directors Speak* (Chicago: Regnery, 1969), p. 248.

15. Quoted in Ed Sigov, *On Sunset Boulevard: The Life and Times of Billy Wilder* (New York: Hyperion, 1998), p. 203.

16. Jay Leyda, ed., *Voices of Film Experience: 1894 to the Present* (New York: Macmillan, 1977), p. 509.

17. Eric Lax, *Woody Allen: A Biography* (1991; New York: Vintage, 1992), pp. 37–38.

DOUBLE INDEMNITY

DOUBLE INDEMNITY

Billy Wilder
Raymond Chandler
September 25, 1943

CAST

WALTER NEFF........................FRED MacMURRAY

PHYLLIS DIETRICHSON................BARBARA STANWYCK

BARTON KEYES......................EDWARD G. ROBINSON

LOLA DIETRICHSON..................JEAN HEATHER

MR. DIETRICHSON...................TOM POWERS

NINO ZACHETTE.....................BYRON BARR

MR. NORTON........................RICHARD GAINES

MR. JACKSON.......................PORTER HALL

SAM GORLOPIS......................FORTUNIO BONANOVA

* * *

SEQUENCE "A"

FADE IN:

A-1 LOS ANGELES - A DOWNTOWN INTERSECTION

It is night, about two o'clock, very light traffic.

At the left and in the immediate foreground a semaphore traffic signal stands at GO. Approaching it at about thirty miles per hour is a Dodge 1938 coupe. It is driven erratically and weaving a little, but not out of control.

When the car is about forty feet away, the signal changes to STOP. Car makes no attempt to stop but comes on through.

A-2 A LIGHT NEWSPAPER TRUCK

is crossing the intersection at right angles. It swerves and skids to avoid the Dodge, which goes on as though nothing had happened. The truck stops with a panicky screech of tires. There is a large sign on the truck: "READ THE LOS ANGELES TIMES". The truck driver's infuriated face stares after the coupe.

A-3 THE COUPE

continues along the street, still weaving, then slows down and pulls over towards the curb in front of a tall office building.

A-4 THE COUPE

stops. The headlights are turned off. For a second nothing happens, then the car door opens slowly. A man eases himself out onto the sidewalk and stands a moment leaning on the open door to support himself. He's a tall man, about thirty-five years old. From the way he moves there seems to be something wrong with his left shoulder.

He straightens up and painfully lowers his left hand into his jacket pocket. He leans into the car. He brings out a light-weight overcoat and drapes it across his shoulders. He shuts the car door and walks toward the building.

A-5 ENTRANCE OF THE BUILDING

Above the closed, double-plate glass doors is lettered: "PACIFIC BUILDING". To the left of entrance there is a drugstore, closed, dark except for a faint light in the back. The man comes stiffly up to the doors. (CAMERA HAS MOVED UP WITH HIM). He tries the doors. They are locked. He knocks on the glass. Inside, over his shoulder, the lobby of the building is visible: a side entrance to the drugstore on the left, in the rear a barber shop and cigar and magazine stand closed up for the night, and to the right two elevators. One elevator is open and its dome light falls across the dark lobby.

9-25-43   (Continued)

A-5 (Cont'd)

The man knocks again. The night watchman sticks his head out of the elevator and looks toward entrance. He comes out with a newspaper in one hand and a half-eaten sandwich in the other. He finishes the sandwich on the way to the doors, looks out and recognizes the man outside, unlocks the door and pulls it open.

NIGHT
WATCHMAN: Hello there, Mr. Neff.

Neff walks in past him without answering.

A-6   INT. LOBBY

Neff is walking towards elevator. Night watchman looks after him, relocks door, follows to elevator. Neff enters elevator.

A-7   ELEVATOR

Neff stands leaning against wall. He is pale and haggard with pain, but deadpans as night watchman joins him.

NIGHT
WATCHMAN: Working pretty late aren't you, Mr. Neff?

NEFF: (Tight-lipped)
          Late enough.

NIGHT
WATCHMAN: You look kind of all in at that.

NEFF: I'm fine. Let's ride.

Night watchman pulls lever, doors close and elevator rises.

NIGHT
WATCHMAN: How's the insurance business,
          Mr. Neff?

NEFF: Okay.

NIGHT
WATCHMAN: They wouldn't ever sell me any. They
          say I've got something loose in my
          heart. I say it's rheumatism.

NEFF: (Scarcely listening)
          Uh-huh.

Night watchman looks around at him, turns away again and the elevator stops.

NIGHT
WATCHMAN: (Surly)
          Twelve.

9-25-43

(Continued)

A-7   (Cont'd)

The door opens. Across a small dark reception room a pair
of frosted glass doors are lettered: PACIFIC ALL-RISK
INSURANCE COMPANY - FOUNDED 1906 - MAIN OFFICE. There is
a little light beyond the glass doors.

Neff straightens up and walks heavily out of the elevator,
across reception room to doors. He pushes them open. The
night watchman stares after him morosely, works lever, elevator doors start to close.

A-8   TWELFTH FLOOR INSURANCE OFFICE

(Note for set-designer: Our Insurance Company occupies the
entire eleventh and twelfth floors of the building. On the
twelfth floor are the executive offices and claims and sales
departments. These all open off a balcony which runs all
the way around. From the balcony you see the eleventh floor
below: one enormous room filled with desks, typewriters,
filing cabinets, business machines, etc.)

Neff comes through the double entrance doors from the reception room. The twelfth floor is dark. Some light shines
up from the eleventh floor. Neff takes a few steps then
holds on to the balcony railing and looks down.

A-9   THE ELEVENTH FLOOR FROM ABOVE - NEFF'S POINT OF VIEW

Two colored women are cleaning the offices. One is dry-
mopping the floor, the other is moving chairs back into position, etc. A colored man is emptying waste baskets into a
big square box. He shuffles a little dance step as he moves,
and hums a little tune.

A-10   NEFF

Moves away from the railing with a faint smile on his face,
and walks past two or three offices (CAMERA WITH HIM) towards
a glass door with number twenty-seven on it and three names:
HENRY B. ANDERSON, WALTER NEFF, LOUIS L. SCHWARTZ. Neff
opens the door.

A-11   INT. NEFF'S OFFICE - DARK

Three desks, filing cabinets, one typewriter on stand, one
dictaphone on fixed stand against wall with rack of records
underneath, telephones on all three desks. Water cooler with
inverted bottle and paper cup holder beside it. Two windows
facing toward front of building. Venetian blinds. No curtains. Waste basket full, ash trays not emptied. The office
has not been cleaned.

Neff enters, switches on desk lamp. He looks across at dicta
phone, goes heavily to it and lifts off the fabric cover. He
leans down hard on the dictaphone stand as if feeling faint.
He turns away from dictaphone, takes a few uncertain steps and
falls heavily into a swivel chair. His head goes far back, hi

9-25-43   (Continued)

A-11 (Cont'd)

eyes close, cold sweat shows on his face. For a moment he
stays like this, exhausted, then his eyes open slowly and
look down at his left shoulder. His good hand flips the
overcoat back, he unbuttons his jacket, loosens his tie and
shirt. This was quite an effort. He rests for a second,
breathing hard. With the help of his good hand he edges
his left elbow up on the arm-rest of the chair, supports it
there and then pulls his jacket wide. A heavy patch of dark
blood shows on his shirt. He pushes his chair along the floor
towards the water cooler, using his feet and his right hand
against the desk, takes out a handkerchief, presses with his
hand against the spring faucet of the cooler, soaks the handkerchief in water and tucks it, dripping wet, against the
wound inside his shirt. Next, he gets a handful of water and
splashes it on his face. The water runs down his chin and
drips. He breathes heavily, with closed eyes. He fingers a
pack of cigarettes in his shirt pocket, pulls it out, looks
at it. There is blood on it. He wheels himself back to the
desk and dumps the loose cigarettes out of the packet. Some
are blood-stained, a few are clean. He takes one, puts it
between his lips, gropes around for a match, lights cigarette.
He takes a deep drag and lets smoke out through his nose.

He pulls himself toward dictaphone again, still in the swivel
chair, reaches it, lifts the horn off the bracket and the
dictaphone makes a low buzzing sound. He presses the button
switch on the horn. The sound stops, the record revolves on
the cylinder. He begins to speak:

NEFF: Office memorandum, Walter Neff to
                     Barton Keyes, Claims Manager.
                     Los Angeles, July 16th, 1938.
                     Dear Keyes: I suppose you'll call
                     this a confession when you hear it.
                     I don't like the word confession.
                     I just want to set you right about one
                     thing you couldn't see, because it was
                     smack up against your nose. You think
                     you're such a hot potato as a claims
                     manager, such a wolf on a phoney claim.
                     Well, maybe you are, Keyes, but let's
                     take a look at this Dietrichson claim,
                     Accident and Double Indemnity. You
                     were pretty good in there for a while,
                     all right. You said it wasn't an
                     accident. Check. You said it wasn't
                     suicide. Check. You said it was murder.
                     Check and double check. You thought
                     you had it cold, all wrapped up in tissue
                     paper, with pink ribbons around it. It
                     was perfect, except that it wasn't,
                     because you made a mistake, just one
                     tiny little mistake. When it came to
                     picking the killer, you picked the wrong

(Continued)

A-11 (Cont'd)

> NEFF: guy, if you know what I mean. Want
> (Cont'd)   to know who killed Dietrichson? Hold
>   tight to that cheap cigar of yours,
>   Keyes. I killed Dietrichson. Me,
>   Walter Neff, insurance agent, 35
>   years old, unmarried, no visible
>   scars -
>   (He glances down at his
>   wounded shoulder)
>   until a little while ago, that is.
>   Yes, I killed him. I killed him for
>   money - and a woman - and I didn't
>   get the money and I didn't get the
>   woman. Pretty, isn't it?

He interrupts the dictation, lays down the horn on the desk.
He takes his lighted cigarette from the ash tray, puffs it
two or three times, and kills it. He picks up the horn again.

> NEFF: (His voice is now quiet
>   and contained)
>   It began last May. About the end of
>   May, it was. I had to run out to
>   Glendale to deliver a policy on some
>   dairy trucks. On the way back I remem-
>   bered this auto renewal on Los Feliz.
>   So I decided to run over there. It was one of those
>   Calif. Spanish houses everyone was nuts about 10 or 15 years ago, This one must have
>   cost somebody about 30,000 bucks - that is, if he ever finished paying for it.

As he goes on speaking,

SLOW DISSOLVE TO:

A-12 DIETRICHSON HOME -
      LOS FELIZ DISTRICT   NEFF'S VOICE

Palm trees line the street,   It was mid-afternoon, and
middle-class houses, mostly
in Spanish style. Some kids   it's funny, I can still
throwing a baseball back and
forth across a couple of front   remember the smell of
lawns. An ice cream wagon
dawdles along the block.   honeysuckle all along that
Neff's coupe meets and passes
the ice cream wagon and stops   block. I felt like a
before one of the Spanish
houses. Neff gets out.   million. There was no way

He carries a briefcase, his   in all this world I could
hat is a little on the back
of his head. His movements   have known that murder
are easy and full of ginger.
He inspects the house, checks   sometimes can smell like
the number, goes up on the
front porch and rings the   honeysuckle.....
bell.

A-13   <u>EXT. DIETRICHSON HOME</u> - ENTRANCE DOOR

Neff rings the bell again and waits. The door opens. A maid, about forty-five, rather slatternly, opens the door.

NEFF: Mr. Dietrichson in?

MAID: Who wants to see him?

NEFF: The name is Neff. Walter Neff.

MAID: If you're selling something---

NEFF: Look, it's Mr. Dietrichson I'd like
                    to talk to, and it's not magazine
                    subscriptions.

He pushes past her into the house.

A-14   <u>HALLWAY</u> - DIETRICHSON HOME

Spanish craperoo in style, as is the house throughout. A wrought-iron staircase curves down from the second floor. A fringed Mexican shawl hangs down over the landing. A large tapestry hangs on the wall. Downstairs, the dining room to one side, living room on the other side visible through a wide archway. All of this, architecture, furniture, decorations, etc., is genuine early Leo Carrillo period. Neff has edged his way in past maid who still holds the door open.

MAID: Listen, Mr. Dietrichson's not in.

NEFF: How soon do you expect him?

MAID: He'll be home when he gets here,
                    if that's any help to you.

At this point a voice comes from the top of the stairs.

VOICE: What is it, Nettie? Who is it?

Neff looks up.

A-15   <u>UPPER LANDING OF STAIRCASE</u> - (FROM BELOW)

Phyllis Dietrichson stands looking down. She is in her early thirties. She holds a large bath-towel around her very appetizing torso, down to about two inches above her knees. She wears no stockings, no nothing. On her feet a pair of high-heeled bedroom slippers with pom-poms. On her left ankle a gold anklet.

MAID'S   It's for Mr. Dietrichson.
VOICE:

9-25-43

                                       (Continued)

PHYLLIS: (Looking down at Neff)
                           I'm Mrs. Dietrichson. What is it?

A-16   SHOOTING DOWN FROM UPPER LANDING

Neff looks up, takes his hat off.

NEFF: How do you do, Mrs. Dietrichson.
                           I'm Walter Neff, Pacific All-Risk.

A-17   PHYLLIS

PHYLLIS: Pacific all-what?

A-18   NEFF

NEFF: Pacific All-Risk Insurance Company.
                           It's about some renewals on the
                           automobiles, Mrs. Dietrichson. I've
                           been trying to contact your husband
                           for the past two weeks. He's never
                           at his office.

A-19   PHYLLIS

PHYLLIS: Is there anything I can do?

A-20   NEFF

NEFF: The insurance ran out on the fifteenth.
                           I'd hate to think of your getting a
                           smashed fender or something while you're
                           not fully covered.

A-21   PHYLLIS

She glances over her towel costume.

PHYLLIS: (With a little smile)
                           Perhaps I know what you mean, Mr.
                           Neff. I've just been taking a sun bath.

A-22   NEFF

NEFF: No pigeons around, I hope . . .About
                           those policies, Mrs. Dietrichson -- I
                           hate to take up your time --

A-23   PHYLLIS

PHYLLIS: That's all right. If you can wait till
                           I put something on, I'll be right down.
                           Nettie, show Mr. Neff into the living room.

A-23 (Cont'd)

She turns away as gracefully as one can with a towel for a wrapper.

A-24   ENTRANCE HALL

Neff watches Phyllis out of sight. He speaks to the maid while still looking up.

NEFF: Where would the living room be?

MAID: In there, but they keep the liquor locked up.

NEFF: That's okay. I always carry my own keys.

He goes through the archway. Maid goes off the other way.

A-25   LIVING ROOM   NEFF'S VOICE

Neff comes into the room and throws his briefcase on the plush davenport and tosses his hat on top of it. He looks around the room, then moves over to a baby grand piano with a sleazy Spanish shawl dangling down one side and two cabinet photographs standing in a staggered position on top. Neff glances them over: Mr. Dietrichson, age about fifty-one, a big, blocky man with glasses and a Rotarian look about him; Lola Dietrichson, age nineteen, wearing a filmy party dress and a yearning look in her pretty eyes. Neff walks away from the piano and takes a few steps back and forth across the rug. His eyes fall on a wrinkled corner. He carefully straightens it out with his foot. His back is to the archway as he hears high heels clicking on the staircase. He turns and looks through the arch.

The living room was still stuffy from last night's cigars. The windows were closed and the sunshine coming in through the Venetian blinds showed up the dust in the air. The furniture was kind of corny and old-fashioned, but it had a comfortable look, as if people really sat in it. On the piano, in couple of fancy frames, were Mr. Dietrichson and Lola, his daughter by his first wife They had a bowl of those little red goldfish on the table behind the davenport, but, to tell you the truth, Keyes, I wasn't a whole lot interested in goldfish right then, nor in auto renewals, nor in Mr. Dietrichson and his daughter Lola. I was thinking about that dame upstairs, and the way she had looked at me, and I wanted to see her again, close, without that silly staircase between us.

A-26   STAIRCASE (FROM NEFF'S POINT OF VIEW)

Phyllis Dietrichson is coming downstairs. First we see her feet, with pompom slippers and the gold anklet on her left ankle. CAMERA PULLS BACK SLOWLY as she descends, until we see all of her. She is wearing a pale blue summer dress.

(Continued)

14

A-26   (Cont'd)

PHYLLIS'
VOICE: I wasn't long, was I?

NEFF'S
VOICE: Not at all, Mrs. Dietrichson.

CAMERA PULLS BACK WITH HER INTO <u>THE LIVING ROOM</u>.

PHYLLIS: I hope I've got my face on straight.

NEFF: It's perfect for my money.

PHYLLIS: (Crossing to the mirror
                       over the fireplace)
            Won't you sit down, Mr. -- Neff is
            the name, isn't it?

NEFF: With two f's, like in Philadelphia.
            If you know the story.

PHYLLIS: What story?

NEFF: The Philadelphia story. What are
            we talking about?

PHYLLIS: (She works with her lipstick)
            About the insurance. My husband never
            tells me anything.

NEFF: It's on your two cars, the La Salle
            and the Plymouth.

He crosses to the davenport to get the policies from his
briefcase. She turns away from the mirror and sits in a big
chair with her legs drawn up sideways, the anklet now
clearly visible.

NEFF: We've been handling this insurance for
            three years for Mr. Dietrichson...
               (His eyes have caught the anklet)
            That's a honey of an anklet you're
            wearing, Mrs. Dietrichson.

Phyllis smiles faintly and covers the anklet with her dress.

NEFF: We'd hate to see the policies lapse.
            Of course, we give him thirty days.
            That's all we're allowed to give.

PHYLLIS: I guess he's been too busy down at
            Long Beach in the oil fields.

9-25-43

                                            (Continued)

A-26   (Cont'd)

NEFF: Could I catch him home some evening for a few minutes?

PHYLLIS: I suppose so. But he's never home much before eight.

NEFF: That would be fine with me.

PHYLLIS: You're not connected with the Automobile Club, are you?

NEFF: No, the All-Risk, Mrs. Dietrichson. Why?

PHYLLIS: Somebody from the Automobile Club has been trying to get him. Do they have a better rate?

NEFF: If your husband's a member.

PHYLLIS: No, he isn't.

Phyllis rises and walks up and down, paying less and less attention.

NEFF: Well, he'd have to join the club and pay a membership fee to start with. The Automobile Club is fine. I never knock the other fellow's merchandise, Mrs. Dietrichson, but I can do just as well for you. I have a very attractive policy here. It wouldn't take me two minutes to put it in front of your husband.

He consults the policies he is holding.

NEFF: For instance, we're writing a new kind of fifty percent retention feature in the collision coverage.

Phyllis stops in her walk.

PHYLLIS: You're a smart insurance man, aren't you, Mr. Neff?

NEFF: I've had eleven years of it.

PHYLLIS: Doing pretty well?

A-26   (Cont'd)

NEFF: It's a living.

PHYLLIS: You handle just automobile insurance,
or all kinds?

She sits down again, in the same position as before.

NEFF: All kinds. Fire, earthquake, theft,
public liability, group insurance,
industrial stuff and so on right down
the line.

PHYLLIS: Accident insurance?

NEFF: Accident insurance? Sure, Mrs. Dietrichson.

His eyes fall on the anklet again.

NEFF: I wish you'd tell me what's engraved
on that anklet.

PHYLLIS: Just my name.

NEFF: As for instance?

PHYLLIS: Phyllis.

NEFF: Phyllis. I think I like that.

PHYLLIS: But you're not sure?

NEFF: I'd have to drive it around the block
a couple of times.

PHYLLIS: (Standing up again)
Mr. Neff, why don't you drop by tomorrow
evening about eight-thirty. He'll be in
then.

NEFF: Who?

PHYLLIS: My husband. You were anxious to talk
to him weren't you?

NEFF: Sure, only I'm getting over it a little.
If you know what I mean.

PHYLLIS: There's a speed limit in this state, Mr.
Neff. Forty-five miles an hour.

NEFF: How fast was I going, officer?

A-26 (Cont'd)

PHYLLIS: I'd say about ninety.

NEFF: Suppose you get down off your motor-cycle and give me a ticket.

PHYLLIS: Suppose I let you off with a warning this time.

NEFF: Suppose it doesn't take.

PHYLLIS: Suppose I have to whack you over the knuckles.

NEFF: Suppose I bust out crying and put my head on your shoulder.

PHYLLIS: Suppose you try putting it on my husband's shoulder.

NEFF: That tears it.

Neff takes his hat and briefcase.

NEFF: Eight-thirty tomorrow evening then, Mrs. Dietrichson.

PHYLLIS: That's what I suggested.

They both move toward the archway.

A-27   <u>HALLWAY</u> - PHYLLIS AND NEFF GOING TOWARDS THE <u>ENTRANCE DOOR</u>

NEFF: Will you be here, too?

PHYLLIS: I guess so. I usually am.

NEFF: Same chair, same perfume, same anklet?

PHYLLIS: (Opening the door)
          I wonder if I know what you mean.

NEFF: I wonder if you wonder.

He walks out.

A-28   <u>EXT. DIETRICHSON HOME</u> - (DAY)

Shooting past Neff's parked car towards the entrance door, which is just closing. Neff comes to-wards the car, swinging his brief-case. He opens the car door and looks back with a confident smile.

                 NEFF'S VOICE
                (Over scene)
She liked me. I could feel that. The way you feel when the cards are

9-25-43   (Continued)

A-29 ENTRANCE DOOR, DIETRICHSON HOME

In the upper panel the peep window opens and Phyllis looks out after Neff.

A-30 NEFF

He sits in his car, presses the starter button, looking back towards the little window in the entrance door.

A-31 ENTRANCE DOOR

The peep window is quickly closed from inside.

A-32 STREET

Neff makes a U-turn and drives back down the block.

DISSOLVE TO:

A-33 LONG SHOT - INSURANCE OFFICE - TWELFTH FLOOR - (DAY) - CAMERA HIGH

Activity on the eleventh floor below. Typewriters working, adding machines, filing clerks, secretaries, and so forth. Neff, wearing his hat and carrying his briefcase, enters from the vestibule. He walks towards his office. He passes a few salesmen, etc. There is an exchange of greetings. Just as he reaches his office a secretary comes out. She stops.

NEFF'S VOICE
(Cont'd)
falling right for you, with a nice little pile of blue and yellow chips in the middle of the table. Only what I didn't know then was that I wasn't playing her. She was playing me -- with a deck of marked cards -- and the stakes weren't any blue and yellow chips. They were dynamite. I went back to the office that afternoon to see if I had any mail. It was the same afternoon you had that Sam Gorlopis on the carpet, that truck driver from Inglewood, remember, Keyes?

SECRETARY: Oh, Mr. Neff, Mr. Keyes wants to see you. He's been yelling for you all afternoon.

NEFF: Is he sore, or just frothing at the mouth a little? Here, park these for me, sweetheart.

He hands her his hat and briefcase and continues right on, CAMERA WITH HIM, to a door lettered:

BARTON KEYES - CLAIMS MANAGER

Keyes' voice is heard inside, plenty loud. Neff grins as he opens the door and goes in.

9-27-43

A-34   <u>KEYES' OFFICE</u> - (DAY)

A minor executive office, not too tidy: large desk across one
corner, good carpet, several chairs, filing cabinet against
one wall, a dictaphone on the corner of the desk.

Keyes is sitting behind the desk with his coat off but his
hat on. A cigar is clamped in his mouth, ashes falling like
snow down his vest, a gold chair and elk's tooth across it.
On the other side of the desk sits Sam Gorlopis. He is a
big, dumb bruiser, six feet three inches tall - a dirty work
shirt and corduroy pants, rough, untidy hair, broad face,
small piggish eyes. He holds a sweat-soaked hat on his knee
with a hairy hand. He is chewing gum rapidly. As Neff opens
the door, Keyes is giving it to Gorlopis.

KEYES: Wise up, Gorlopis. You're not
                   kidding anybody with that line
                   of bull. You're in a jam and
                   you know it.

GORLOPIS: Sez you. All I want is my money.

KEYES: Sez you. All you're gonna get
                   is the cops.

He sees Neff standing inside the door.

KEYES: Come in, Walter. This is Sam
                   Gorlopis from Inglewood.

NEFF: Sure, I know Mr. Gorlopis.
                   Wrote a policy on his truck.
                   How are you, Mr. Gorlopis?

GORLOPIS: I ain't so good. My truck burned
                   down.

He looks cautiously sideways at Keyes.

KEYES: Yeah, he just planted his big foot
                   on the starter and the whole thing
                   blazed up in his face.

GORLOPIS: Yes, sir.

KEYES: And didn't even singe his eyebrows.

GORLOPIS: No sir. Look, mister. I got twenty-
                   six hundred bucks tied up in that truck.
                   I'm insured with this company and I want
                   my money.

KEYES: You got a wife, Gorlopis?

GORLOPIS: Sure I got a wife.

KEYES: You got kids?

A-34 (Cont'd)

GORLOPIS: Two kids.

KEYES: What you got for dinner tonight?

GORLOPIS: We got meat loaf.

KEYES: How do you make your meat loaf, Gorlopis?

GORLOPIS: Veal and pork and bread and garlic. Greek style.

KEYES: How much garlic?

GORLOPIS: Lotsa garlic, Mr. Keyes.

KEYES: Okay, Gorlopis. Now listen here. Let's say you just came up here to tell me how to make meat loaf. That's all, understand? Because if you came up here to claim on that truck, I'd have to turn you over to the law, Gorlopis, and they'd put you in jail. No wife. No kids --

GORLOPIS: What for?

KEYES: (Yelling) And no meat loaf, Gorlopis!

GORLOPIS: I didn't do nothin'.

KEYES: No? Look, Gorlopis. Every month hundreds of claims come to this desk. Some of them are phonies, and I know which ones. How do I know, Gorlopis? (He speaks as if to a child) Because my little man tells me.

GORLOPIS: What little man?

KEYES: The little man in here.

He pounds the pit of his stomach.

KEYES: Everytime one of those phonies comes along he ties knots in my stomach. And yours was one of them, Gorlopis. That's how I knew your claim was crooked. So what did I do? I sent a tow car out to your garage this afternoon and they jacked up that burned-out truck of yours. And what did they find, Gorlopis? They found what was left of a pile of shavings.

9-27-43   (Continued)

A-34 (Cont'd)

GORLOPIS: What shavings?

KEYES: The ones you soaked with kerosene
                      and dropped a match on.

Gorlopis cringes under the impact.

GORLOPIS: Look, Mr. Keyes, I'm just a poor
                      guy. Maybe I made a mistake.

KEYES: That's one way of putting it.

GORLOPIS: I ain't feelin' so good, Mr. Keyes.

KEYES: Sign this and you'll feel fine.

He puts a blank form in front of him and points.

KEYES: Right there. It's a waiver on your
                      claim.

Gorlopis hesitates, then signs laboriously.

KEYES: Now you're an honest man again.

GORLOPIS: But I ain't got no more truck.

KEYES: Goodbye, Gorlopis.

GORLOPIS: (Still bewildered)
                      Goodbye, Mr. Keyes.

He stands up and goes slowly to the door and turns there.

GORLOPIS: Twenty-six hundred bucks. That's a
                      lot of dough where I live.

KEYES: What's the matter, Gorlopis? Don't
                      you know how to open the door? Just
                      put your hand on the knob, turn it to
                      the right, pull it toward you --

GORLOPIS: (Doing just as Keyes says)
                      Like this, Mr. Keyes?

KEYES: That's the boy. Now the same thing
                      from the outside.

GORLOPIS: (Stupefied)
                      Thank you, Mr. Keyes.

He goes out, closing the door after him. Keyes takes his
cigar stub from his mouth and turns it slowly in the flame
of a lighted match. He turns to Neff.

9-27-43   (Continued)

A-34   (Cont'd)

KEYES: What kind of an outfit is this anyway?
                Are we an insurance company, or a bunch
                of dimwitted amateurs, writing a policy
                on a mugg like that?

NEFF: Wait a minute, Keyes. I don't rate this
                beef. I clipped a note to that Gorlopis
                application to have him thoroughly inves-
                tigated before we accepted the risk.

KEYES: I know you did, Walter. I'm not beef-
                ing at you. It's the company. The way
                they do things. The way they don't do
                things. The way they'll write anything
                just to get it down on the sales sheet.
                And I'm the guy that has to sit here up
                to my neck in phony claims so they won't
                throw more money out of the window than
                they take in at the door.

NEFF: (Grinning)
                Okay, turn the record over and let's
                hear the other side.

KEYES: I get darn sick of picking up after a
                gang of fast-talking salesmen dumb enough
                to sell life insurance to a guy that
                sleeps in the same bed with four rattle-
                snakes. I've had twenty-six years of that,
                Walter, and I --

NEFF: And you loved every minute of it, Keyes.
                You love it, only you worry about it too
                much, you and your little man. You're
                so darn conscientious you're driving your-
                self crazy. You wouldn't even say today
                is Tuesday without you looked at the
                calendar, and then you would check if it
                was this year's or last year's calendar,
                and then you would find out what company
                printed the calendar, then find out if
                their calendar checks with the World
                Almanac's calendar.

KEYES: That's enough from you, Walter. Get out
                of here before I throw my desk at you.

NEFF: I love you, too.

He walks out, still grinning.

9-27-43

23

A-35   EXT. OFFICES - TWELFTH FLOOR

Neff comes out of Keys' office and walks back along the balcony. Activity of secretaries going in and out of doors, etc. Neff enters his own office.

A-36   INT. NEFF'S OFFICE

Anderson, a salesman, sits at one of the desks, filling out a report. Neff enters, goes to his own desk. He looks down at some mail. On top there is a typewritten note. He reads it, sits down and leafs through his desk calendar.

A-37   INSERT - CLOSEUP - CALENDAR PAGE

Showing date:

> THURSDAY
> 23
> May

and five or six appointments pencilled in tightly on the page.

DISSOLVE TO:

A-38   DIETRICHSON HOME - ENTRANCE HALL - (DAY)

THE CAMERA PANS with Phyllis Dietrichson's feet and ankles as she comes down the stairs, her high heels clicking on the tiles. The anklet glistens on her leg as she moves. THE CAMERA PANS ON. Phyllis has reached the entrance hall, and as she walks toward the front door her whole body becomes visible. She wears a gay print dress with a wide sash over her hips. She opens the door. Outside is Neff, wearing a sport coat, flannel slacks. He takes his hat off.

PHYLLIS: Hello, Mr. Neff.

He stands there with a little smile.

PHYLLIS: Aren't you coming in?

NEFF: I'm considering it.

He comes in.

NEFF'S VOICE
(Over scene)

I really did, too, you old crab, always yelling your fat head off, always sore at everyone. But behind the cigar ashes on your vest I kind of knew you had a heart as big as a house...Back in my office there was a phone message from Mrs. Dietrichson about the renewals. She didn't want me to come tomorrow evening. She wanted me to come Thursday afternoon at three-thirty instead. I had a lot of stuff lined up for that Thursday afternoon, including a trip down to Santa Monica to see a couple of live prospects about some group insurance. But I kept thinking about Phyllis Dietrichson and the way that anklet of hers cut into her leg.

(Continued)

A-38   (Cont'd)

> PHYLLIS: I hope you didn't mind my changing the
>   appointment. Last night wasn't so con-
>   venient.
>
> NEFF: That's okay. I was working on my stamp
>   collection.

She leads him toward living room.

A-39   DIETRICHSON LIVING ROOM

Phyllis and Neff come through archway. She heads toward a
low tea table which stands in front of the davenport, with
tall glasses, ice cubes, lemon, a pot of tea, etc.

> PHYLLIS: I was just fixing some iced tea.
>   Would you like a glass?
>
> NEFF: Unless you have a bottle of beer
>   that's not working.
>
> PHYLLIS: There might be some. I never
>   know what's in the ice box.
>   (Calls)
>   Nettie!....

She pours herself a glass of tea.

> PHYLLIS: About those renewals, Mr. Neff.
>   I talked to my husband about it.
>
> NEFF: You did?
>
> PHYLLIS: Yes. He'll renew with you he told
>   me. In fact, I thought he'd be here
>   this afternoon.
>
> NEFF: But he's not?
>
> PHYLLIS: No.
>
> NEFF: That's terrible.
>
> PHYLLIS: (Calls again, impatiently)
>   Nettie!..Nettie!....Oh, I forgot, it's the
>   maid's day off.
>
> NEFF: Don't bother, Mrs. Dietrichson.
>   I'd like some iced tea very much.
>
> PHYLLIS: Lemon? Sugar?
>
> NEFF: Fix it your way.

9-27-43

(Continued)

A-39 (Cont'd)

She fixes him a glass of tea while he is looking around.
He slowly sits down.

NEFF: Seeing it's the maid's day off
        maybe there's something I can do
        for you.

She hands him the tea.

NEFF: Like running the vacuum cleaner.

PHYLLIS: Fresh.

NEFF: I used to peddle vacuum cleaners. Not
        much money but you learn a lot about life.

PHYLLIS: I didn't think you'd learned it from
        a correspondence course.

NEFF: Where did you pick up this tea drink-
        ing? You're not English, are you?

PHYLLIS: No. Californian. Born right here in
        Los Angeles.

NEFF: They say native Californians all come
        from Iowa.

PHYLLIS: I wanted to ask you something, Mr. Neff.

NEFF: Make it Walter.

PHYLLIS: Walter.

NEFF: Right.

PHYLLIS: Tell me, Walter, on this insurance -
        how much commission do you make?

NEFF: Twenty percent. Why?

PHYLLIS: I thought maybe I could throw a little
        more business your way.

NEFF: I can always use it.

PHYLLIS: I was thinking about my husband. I
        worry a lot about him, down in those
        oil fields. It's very dangerous.

NEFF: Not for an executive, is it?

9-27-43   (Continued)

A-39   (Cont'd)

PHYLLIS: He doesn't just sit behind a desk. He's right down there with the drilling crews. It's got me worried sick.

NEFF: You mean a crown block might fall on him some rainy night?

PHYLLIS: Please don't talk like that.

NEFF: But that's the idea.

PHYLLIS: The other day a casing line snapped and caught the foreman. He's in the hospital with a broken back.

NEFF: Bad.

PHYLLIS: It's got me jittery just thinking about it. Suppose something like that happened to my husband?

NEFF: It could.

PHYLLIS: Don't you think he ought to have accident insurance?

NEFF: Uh huh.

PHYLLIS: What kind of insurance could he have?

NEFF: Enough to cover doctors' and hospital bills. Say a hundred and twenty-five a week cash benefit. And he'd rate around fifty thousand capital sum.

PHYLLIS: Capital sum? What's that?

NEFF: That's if he got killed. Maybe I shouldn't have said that.

PHYLLIS: I suppose you have to think of everything in your business.

NEFF: Mr. Dietrichson would understand. I'm sure I could sell him on the idea of some accident protection. Why don't I talk to him about it.

PHYLLIS: You could try. But he's pretty tough going.

NEFF: They're all tough at first.

9-27-43   (Continued)

A-39   (Cont'd)

PHYLLIS: He's got a lot on his mind. He doesn't want to listen to anything except maybe a baseball game on the radio. Sometimes we sit all evening without saying a word to each other.

NEFF: Sounds pretty dull.

Phyllis shrugs.

PHYLLIS: So I just sit and knit.

NEFF: Is that what you married him for?

PHYLLIS: Maybe I like the way his thumbs hold up the wool.

NEFF: Anytime his thumbs get tired---
                      (Pause)

PHYLLIS: I want to ask you something, Mr. Neff. Could I get an accident policy for him--- without bothering him at all?

NEFF: How's that again.

PHYLLIS: That would make it easier for you, too. You wouldn't even have to talk to him. I have a little allowance of my own. I could pay for it and he needn't know anything about it.

NEFF: Wait a minute. Why shouldn't he know?

PHYLLIS: Because I know he doesn't want accident insurance. He's superstitious about it.

NEFF: A lot of people are. Funny, isn't it?

PHYLLIS: If there was a way to get it like that, all the worry would be over. You see what I mean, Walter?

NEFF: Sure. I've got good eyesight. You want him to have the policy without him know- ing it. And that means without the in- surance company knowing that he doesn't know. That's the set-up, isn't it?

PHYLLIS: Is there anything wrong with it?

NEFF: I think it's lovely. And then, some dark wet night, if that crown block fell on him --

9-27-43   (Continued)

A-39 (Cont'd)

PHYLLIS: What crown block?

NEFF: Only sometimes they have to have a little help. They can't quite make it on their own.

PHYLLIS: I don't know what you're talking about.

NEFF: Of course, it doesn't have to be a crown block. It can be a car backing over him, or he can fall out of an upstairs window. Any little thing like that, as long as it's a morgue job.

PHYLLIS: Are you crazy?

NEFF: Not that crazy. Goodbye, Mrs. Dietrichson.

He picks up his hat.

PHYLLIS: What's the matter?

NEFF: Look, baby, you can't get away with it.

PHYLLIS: Get away with what?

NEFF: You want to knock him off, don't you, baby.

PHYLLIS: That's a horrible thing to say!

NEFF: Who'd you think I was, anyway? A guy that walks into a good-looking dame's front parlor and says "Good afternoon, I sell accident insurance on husbands. You got one that's been around too long? Somebody you'd like to turn into a little hard cash? Just give me a smile and I'll help you collect." Boy, what a dope I must look to you!

PHYLLIS: I think you're rotten.

NEFF: I think you're swell. So long as I'm not your husband.

PHYLLIS: Get out of here.

NEFF: You bet I will. You bet I'll get out of here, baby. But quick.

He goes out. She looks after him.

9-27-43

29

A-40   EXT. DIETRICHSON HOME - (DAY)

Neff bangs the front door
shut, walks quickly to his
car and drives away.

DISSOLVE TO:

A-41   DRIVE-IN RESTAURANT - (DAY)

Shooting past Neff sitting
behind the wheel of his car
The car hop hangs a tray on
the door and serves him a
bottle of beer.

DISSOLVE TO:

A-42   INT. BOWLING ALLEY

Neff bowling. He rolls
the ball with an effort at
concentration, but his
mind is not really on the
game.

DISSOLVE TO:

A-43   EXT. APARTMENT HOUSE - (DUSK)

It is late afternoon. The apartment house is called the LOS OLIVOS
APARTMENTS. It is a six-story
building in the Normandie-Wilshire
district, with a basement garage.
THE CAMERA PANS UP the front of the
building to the top floor windows,
as a little rain starts to fall.

DISSOLVE TO:

A-44   INT. NEFF'S APARTMENT - LIVING
ROOM - (DUSK)

It is a double apartment of con-
ventional design, with kitchen,
dinette, and bathroom, square-
cut overstuffed borax furniture.
Gas logs are lit in the imita-
tion fireplace. Neff stands by
the window with his coat off and
his tie loose. Raindrops strike
against the glass. He turns
away impatiently, paces up and
down past a caddy bag with golf
clubs in it, pulls one out at
random, makes a couple of short
swings, throws the club on the
couch, paces again.

NEFF'S VOICE
(Over scene)
So I let her have it,
straight between the eyes.
She didn't fool me for a
minute, not this time. I
knew I had hold of a red-
hot poker and the time to
drop it was before it
burned my hand off. I
stopped at a drive-in for a
bottle of beer, the one I
had wanted all along, only
I wanted it worse now, to
get rid of the sour taste
of her iced tea, and everything that went with it. I
didn't want to go back to
the office, so I dropped
by a bowling alley at
Third and Western and
rolled a few lines to get
my mind thinking about
something else for a while.

NEFF'S VOICE
(Continuing)
I didn't feel like eat-
ing dinner when I left,
and I didn't feel like
a show, so I drove home,
put the car away and
went up to my apartment.

It had begun to rain
outside and I watched
it get dark and didn't
even turn on the light.
That didn't help me
either. I was all
twisted up inside, and
I was still holding on
to that red-hot poker.
And right then it came
over me that I hadn't
walked out on anything
at all, that the hook
was too strong, that
this wasn't the end be-
tween her and me. It
was only the beginning.
(Continued)

9-27-43

30

A-44 (Cont'd)

The doorbell rings.

Neff goes to the door and opens
it.

> So at eight o'clock the
> bell would ring and I
> would know who it was
> without even having to
> think, as if it was the
> most natural thing in
> the world.

PHYLLIS: Hello.

Neff just looks at her.

PHYLLIS: You forgot your hat this afternoon.

She has nothing in her hands but her bag.

NEFF: Did I?

He looks down at her hands.

PHYLLIS: Don't you want me to bring it in?

NEFF: Sure. Put it on the chair.

She comes in. He closes the door.

NEFF: How did you know where I live?

PHYLLIS: It's in the phone book.

Neff switches on the standing lamp.

PHYLLIS: It's raining.

NEFF: So it is. Peel off your coat and sit
                  down.

She starts to take off her coat.

NEFF: Your husband out?

PHYLLIS: Long Beach. They're spudding in a new
                  well. He phoned he'd be late. About
                  nine-thirty.

He takes her coat and lays it across the back of a chair.

PHYLLIS: It's about time you said you're glad
                  to see me.

NEFF: I knew you wouldn't leave it like that.

PHYLLIS: Like what?

9-27-43   (Continued)

A-44   (Cont'd)

NEFF: Like it was this afternoon.

PHYLLIS: I must have said something that gave
you a terribly wrong impression. You
must surely see that. You must never
think anything like that about me, Walter.

NEFF: Okay.

PHYLLIS: It's not okay. Not if you don't believe me.

NEFF: What do you want me to do?

PHYLLIS: I want you to be nice to me. Like the
first time you came to the house.

NEFF: It can't be like the first time.
Something has happened.

PHYLLIS: I know it has. It's happened to us.

NEFF: That's what I mean.

Phyllis has moved over to the window. She stares out
through the wet window-pane.

NEFF: What's the matter now?

PHYLLIS: I feel as if he was watching me. Not
that he cares about me. Not any more.
But he keeps me on a leash. So tight
I can't breathe. I'm scared.

NEFF: What of? He's in Long Beach, isn't he?

PHYLLIS: I oughtn't to have come.

NEFF: Maybe you oughtn't.

PHYLLIS: You want me to go?

NEFF: If you want to.

PHYLLIS: Right now?

NEFF: Sure. Right now.

By this time, he has hold of her wrist. He draws her to
him slowly and kisses her. Her arms tighten around him.
After a moment he pulls his head back, still holding her
close.

NEFF: How were you going to do it?

9-27-43   (Continued)

A-44   (Cont'd)

PHYLLIS: Do what?

NEFF: Kill him.

PHYLLIS: Walter, for the last time --

She tries to jerk away but he holds her and kisses her again.

NEFF: I'm crazy about you, baby.

PHYLLIS: I'm crazy about you, Walter.

NEFF: That perfume on your hair. What's the name of it?

PHYLLIS: Something French. I bought it down at Ensenada.

NEFF: We ought to have some of that pink wine to go with it. The kind that bubbles. But all I have is bourbon.

PHYLLIS: Bourbon is fine, Walter.

He lets her go and moves toward the dinette.

A-45   THE DINETTE AND KITCHEN

It contains a small table and some chairs. A low glass-and-china cabinet is built between the dinette and kitchen, leaving a space like a doorway. The kitchen is the usual apartment house kitchen, with stove, ice-box, sink, etc. It is quite small.

Neff goes to the ice-box and Phyllis drifts in after him.

NEFF: Soda?

PHYLLIS: Plain water, please.

NEFF: Get a couple of glasses, will you.

He points at the china closet. He has taken a tray of ice cubes from the refrigerator and is holding it under the hot-water faucet.

NEFF: You know, about six months ago a guy slipped on the soap in his bathtub and knocked himself cold and drowned. Only he had accident insurance. So they had an autopsy and she didn't get away with it.

Phyllis has the glasses now. She hands them to him. He dumps some ice cubes into the glasses.

9-27-43

(Continued)

A-45   (Cont'd)

PHYLLIS: Who didn't?

NEFF: His wife.

He reaches for the whiskey bottle on top of the china closet.

                     And there was another case where a guy was found shot and his wife said he was cleaning a gun and his stomach got in the way. All she collected was a three-to-ten stretch in Tehachapi.

PHYLLIS: Perhaps it was worth it to her.

Neff hands her a glass.

NEFF: See if you can carry this as far as the living room.

They move back toward the living room.

A-46   LIVING ROOM

Phyllis and Neff go toward the davenport. She is sipping her drink and looking around.

PHYLLIS: It's nice here, Walter. Who takes care of it for you?

NEFF: A colored woman comes in twice a week.

PHYLLIS: You get your own breakfast?

NEFF: Once in a while I squeeze a grapefruit. The rest I get at the corner drugstore.

They sit on the davenport, fairly close together.

PHYLLIS: It sounds wonderful. Just strangers beside you. You don't know them. You don't hate them. You don't have to sit across the table and smile at him and that daughter of his every morning of your life.

NEFF: What daughter? Oh, that little girl on the piano.

PHYLLIS: Yes. Lola. She lives with us. He thinks a lot more of her than he does of me.

NEFF: Ever think of a divorce?

PHYLLIS: He wouldn't give me a divorce.

A-46 (Cont'd)

NEFF: I suppose because it would cost him money.

PHYLLIS: He hasn't got any money. Not since he
            went into the oil business.

NEFF: But he had when you married him?

PHYLLIS: Yes, he had. And I wanted a home.
            Why not? But that wasn't the only
            reason. I was his wife's nurse. She
            was sick for a long time. When she died,
            he was all broken up. I pitied him so.

NEFF: And now you hate him.

PHYLLIS: Yes, Walter. He's so mean to me. Every-
            time I buy a dress or a pair of shoes he
            yells his head off. He won't let me go
            anywhere. He keeps me shut up. He's al-
            ways been mean to me. Even his life in-
            surance all goes to that daughter of his.
            That Lola.

NEFF: Nothing for you at all, huh?

PHYLLIS: No. And nothing is just what I'm
            worth to him.

NEFF: So you lie awake in the dark and
            listen to him snore and get ideas.

PHYLLIS: Walter, I don't want to kill him. I
            never did. Not even when he gets drunk
            and slaps my face.

NEFF: Only sometimes you wish he was dead.

PHYLLIS: Perhaps I do.

NEFF: And you wish it was an accident, and
            you had that policy. For fifty thousand
            dollars. Is that it?

PHYLLIS: Perhaps that too.

She takes a long drink.

            The other night we drove home from a
            party. He was drunk again. When we
            got into the garage he just sat there
            with his head on the steering wheel and
            the motor still running. And I thought
            what it would be like if I didn't switch
            it off, just closed the garage door and
            left him there.

9-27-43   (Continued)

A-46   (Cont'd)

NEFF: I'll tell you what it would be like,
if you had that accident policy, and
tried to pull a monoxide job. We have
a guy in our office named Keyes. For
him a set-up like that would be just like
a slice of rare roast beef. In three minutes he'd know it wasn't an accident. In
ten minutes you'd be sitting under the hot
lights. In half an hour you'd be signing
your name to a confession.

PHYLLIS: But Walter, I didn't do it. I'm not going
to do it.

NEFF: Not if there's an insurance company in the
picture, baby. So long as you're honest
they'll pay you with a smile, but you just
try to pull something like that and you'll
find out. · They know more tricks than a car-
load of monkeys. And if there's a death
mixed up in it, you haven't got a prayer.
They'll hang you as sure as ten dimes will
buy a dollar, baby.

She begins to cry. He puts his arms around her and kisses
her.

NEFF: Just stop thinking about it, will you.

He holds her tight. Their heads touch, side by side, THE
CAMERA SLOWLY STARTS TO RECEDE as we

DISSOLVE TO:

A-47   <u>INT. NEFF'S OFFICE</u> - (NIGHT)

Neff sits in the swivel chair, talking into the dictaphone.
He has hooked the wastebasket under his feet to sit more
comfortably. As he talks, a little cough shakes him now and
then.

NEFF: So we just sat there, and she kept on
crying softly, like the rain on the
window, and we didn't say anything.
Maybe she had stopped thinking about it,
but I hadn't. I couldn't. Because it all
tied up with something I had been thinking
about for years, since long before I ever
ran into Phyllis Dietrichson. Because, in
this business you can't sleep for trying to
figure out the tricks they could pull on you.
You're like the guy behind the roulette
wheel, watching the customers to make sure

9-27-43

(Continued)

A-47   (Cont'd)

NEFF: they don't crook the house. And then one
(Cont'd)   night, you get to thinking how you could
                crook the house yourself. And do it smart.
                Because you've got that wheel right under
                your hands. And you know every notch in
                it by heart. And you figure all you need
                is a plant out in front, a shill to put
                down the bet. And suddenly the doorbell
                rings and the whole set-up is right there
                in the room with you. . . Look, Keyes, I'm
                not trying to whitewash myself. I fought
                it, only maybe I didn't fight it hard enough.
                The stakes were fifty thousand dollars, but
                they were the life of a man, too, a man
                who'd never done me any dirt. Except he
                was married to a woman he didn't care any-
                thing about, and I did. . .

        DISSOLVE TO:

A-48   INT. NEFF'S APARTMENT LIVING ROOM

CAMERA MOVES SLOWLY towards the davenport again. Neff sits
in one corner with his feet on the low table. He is smoking
his cigarette and staring at the ceiling. Phyllis has been
sitting fairly close to him. She gets up slowly and crosses
to her rain coat, lying over a chair.

PHYLLIS: I've got to go now, Walter.

Neff does not answer. He keeps on staring at the ceiling.
She starts to put the rain coat on.

PHYLLIS: Will you call me, Walter?

Neff still does not answer.

PHYLLIS: Walter!

He looks at her slowly, almost absently.

PHYLLIS: I hate him. I loathe going back
                to him. You believe me, don't you,
                Walter?

NEFF: Sure I believe you.

PHYLLIS: I can't stand it anymore. What
                if they did hang me?

NEFF: You're not going to hang, baby.

PHYLLIS: It's better than going on this way.

9-27-43   (Continued)

A-48 (Cont'd)

NEFF: --- you're not going to hang, baby.
       Not ever. Because you're going to do
       it the smart way. Because I'm going to
       help you.

PHYLLIS: You!

NEFF: Me.

PHYLLIS: Do you know what you're saying?

NEFF: Sure I know what I'm saying.

He gets up and grips her arm.

NEFF: We're going to do it together. We're
       going to do it right. And I'm the
       guy that knows how.

There is fierce determination in his voice. His fingers
dig into her arm.

PHYLLIS: Walter, you're hurting me.

NEFF: There isn't going to be any slip up.
       Nothing sloppy. Nothing weak. It's
       got to be perfect.

He kisses her.

NEFF: You go now.

He leads her towards the door.

NEFF: Call me tomorrow. But not from your house.
       From a booth. And watch your step. Every
       single minute. It's got to be perfect, under-
       stand. Straight down the line.

They have now reached the door. Neff opens it. Phyllis
stands in the doorway, her lips white.

PHYLLIS: Straight down the line.

She goes quietly. He watches her down the corridor. Slowly
he closes the door and goes back into the room. He moves
across the window and opens it wide. He stands there, look-
down into the dark street. From below comes the sound of a
car starting and driving off. The rain drifts in against
his face. He just stands there motionless. His mind is
going a hundred miles a minute.

FADE OUT

      <u>END OF SEQUENCE "A"</u>

9-27-43

SEQUENCE "B"

FADE IN:

B-1   INT. NEFF'S OFFICE - (NIGHT)

Neff sits slumped in his chair before the dictaphone. On
the desk next to him stands a used record. The cylinder on
the dictaphone is not turning. He is smoking a cigarette.
He kills it then lifts the needle and slides off the record
which is on the machine and stands it on end on the desk
beside the other used record. He reaches down painfully to
take another record from the rack beneath the dictaphone,
looks at it against the light to make sure it has not been
used, then slides it into place on the machine and resets
the needle. He lifts the horn and resumes his dictation.

NEFF: The first thing we had to do was fix
                him up with that accident policy. I
                knew he wouldn't buy, but all I wanted
                was his signature on an application.
                So I had to make him sign without his
                knowing what he was signing. And I
                wanted a witness other than Phyllis to
                hear me give him a sales talk. I was
                trying to think with your brains, Keyes.
                I wanted all the answers ready for all
                the questions you were going to spring
                as soon as Dietrichson was dead.

Neff takes a last drag on his cigarette and kills it by running it under the ledge of the dictaphone stand. He drops
the stub on the floor and resumes.

NEFF: A couple of nights later I went to
                the house. Everything looked fine,
                except I didn't like the witness Phyllis
                had brought in. It was Dietrichson's
                daughter Lola, and it made me feel a lit-
                tle queer in the belly to have her right
                there in the room, playing Chinese check-
                ers, as if nothing was going to happen.

DISSOLVE:

B-2   A BOARD OF CHINESE CHECKERS

CAMERA WITHDRAWS AND GRADUALLY REVEALS THE DIETRICHSON LIV-
ING ROOM - NIGHT. The checker-board is on the davenport
between Phyllis and Lola. Mr. Dietrichson sits in a big
easy chair. His coat and tie are over the back of the
chair, and the evening paper is lying tumbled on the floor
beside him. He is smoking a cigar with the band on it.
He has a drink in front of him and several more inside
him. In another chair sits Neff, his briefcase on the
floor, leaning against his chair. He holds his rate book
partly open, with a finger in it for a marker. He is going full swing.

9-30-43   (Continued)

B-2 (Cont'd)

NEFF: I suppose you realize, Mr. Dietrichson,
that, not being an employee, you are not
covered by the State Compensation Insurance Act. The only way you can protect
yourself is by having a personal policy
of your own.

DIETRICHSON: I know all about that. The next thing
you'll tell me I need earthquake insurance
and lightning insurance and hail insurance.

Phyllis looks up from the checker-board and cuts in on the
dialogue. Lola listens without much interest.

PHYLLIS: (To Dietrichson)
If we bought all the insurance they can
think up, we'd stay broke paying for it,
wouldn't we, honey?

DIETRICHSON: What keeps us broke is you going out
and buying five hats at a crack. Who
needs a hat in California?

NEFF: I always say insurance is a lot like a
hot water bottle. It looks kind of
useless and silly hanging on the hook,
but when you get that stomach ache in
the middle of the night, it comes in
mighty handy.

DIETRICHSON: Now you want to sell me a hot water
bottle.

NEFF: Dollar for dollar, accident insurance
is the cheapest coverage you can buy,
Mr. Dietrichson.

DIETRICHSON: Maybe some other time, Mr. Neff. I
had a tough day.

NEFF: Just as you say, Mr. Dietrichson.

DIETRICHSON: Suppose we just settle that automobile insurance tonight.

NEFF: Sure. All we need on that is for you
to sign an application for renewal.

Phyllis throws a quick glance at Neff. As she looks back
she sees that Lola is staring down at her wrist watch.

LOLA: Phyllis, do you mind if we don't
finish this game? It bores me stiff.

9-30-43   (Continued)

B-2 (Cont'd)

PHYLLIS: Got something better to do?

LOLA: Yes, I have.

She gets up.

LOLA: (To Dietrichson)
                    Father, is it all right if I run
                    along now?

DIETRICHSON: Run along where? Who with?

LOLA: Just Anne. We're going roller
                    skating.

DIETRICHSON: Anne who?

LOLA: Anne Matthews.

PHYLLIS: It's not that Nino Zacchetti again?

DIETRICHSON: It better not be that Zacchetti guy.
                    If I ever catch you with that ---

LOLA: It's Anne Matthews, I told you. I
                    also told you we're going roller skat-
                    ing. I'm meeting her at the corner of
                    Vermont and Franklin -- the north-west
                    corner, in case you're interested. And
                    I'm late already. I hope that is all
                    clear. Good night, Father. Good night,
                    Phyllis.

She starts to go.

NEFF: Good night, Miss Dietrichson.

LOLA: Oh, I'm sorry. Good night, Mr. --

NEFF: Neff.

LOLA: Good night, Mr. Neff.

PHYLLIS: Now you're not going to take my
                    car again.

LOLA: No thanks. I'd rather be dead.

She goes out through the archway.

DIETRICHSON: A great little fighter for her
                    weight.

Dietrichson sucks down a big swallow of his drink.

9-30-43   (Continued)

B-2 (Cont'd)

Neff has taken two blank forms from his briefcase. He puts the briefcase on Mr. Dietrichson's lap and lays the forms on top. Phyllis is watching closely.

NEFF: This is where you sign, Mr. Dietrichson.

DIETRICHSON: Sign what?

NEFF: The applications for your auto renewals. So you'll be protected until the new policies are issued.

DIETRICHSON: When will that be?

NEFF: In about a week.

DIETRICHSON: Just so I'm covered when I drive up North.

Neff takes out his fountain pen.

NEFF: San Francisco, Mr. Dietrichson?

DIETRICHSON: Palo Alto.

PHYLLIS: He was a Stanford man, Mr. Neff. And he still goes to his class reunion every year.

DIETRICHSON: What's wrong with that? Can't I have a little fun even once a year?

NEFF: Great football school, Stanford. Did you play football, Mr. Dietrichson?

DIETRICHSON: Left guard. Almost made the varsity, too.

Neff has unscrewed his fountain pen. He hands it to Mr. Dietrichson. Dietrichson puts on his glasses.

NEFF: On that bottom line, Mr. Dietrichson.

Dietrichson signs. Neff's and Phyllis' eyes meet for a split second.

NEFF: Both copies, please.

He withdraws the top copy barely enough to expose the signature line on the supposed duplicate.

DIETRICHSON: Sign twice, huh?

9-30-43

(Continued)

B-2   (Cont'd)

NEFF: One is the agent's copy. I need
it for my files.

DIETRICHSON: (In a mutter)
Files. Duplicates. Triplicates.

Dietrichson grunts and signs again. Again Neff and
Phyllis exchange a quick glance.

NEFF: No hurry about the check, Mr.
Dietrichson. I can pick it up
at your office some morning.

Casually Neff lifts the briefcase and signed applications
off Dietrichson's lap.

DIETRICHSON: How much you taking me for?

NEFF: One forty-seven fifty, Mr.
Dietrichson.

Dietrichson stands up. He is about Neff's height but a
little heavier.

PHYLLIS: I guess that's enough insurance
for one evening, Mr. Neff.

DIETRICHSON: Plenty.

Dietrichson has poured some more whisky into his glass.
He tries the siphon but it is empty. He gathers up his
coat and tie and picks up his glass.

DIETRICHSON: Good night, Mr. Neff.

Neff is zipping up his briefcase.

NEFF: Good night, Mr. Dietrichson.
Good night, Mrs. Dietrichson.

DIETRICHSON: Bring me some soda when you come
up, Phyllis.

Dietrichson trundles off towards the archway.

PHYLLIS: (To Neff)
I think you left your hat in the hall.

Phyllis leads the way and Neff goes after her, his briefcase under his arm.

B-3   <u>HALLWAY DIETRICHSON RESIDENCE</u> - (NIGHT)

Phyllis enters through the living room archway with Neff
behind her. She leads him towards the door. On the way
he picks up his hat. In the BACKGROUND Dietrichson begins to ascend the stairs, carrying his coat and glass.
Phyllis and Neff move close to the door. They speak in
very low voices.

PHYLLIS: All right, Walter?

NEFF: Fine.

PHYLLIS: He signed it, didn't he?

NEFF: Sure he signed it. You saw him.

Phyllis opens the door a crack. Both look at the stairs,
where Dietrichson is going up. Phyllis takes her hand off
the doorknob and holds on to Neff's arm.

NEFF: (Looking up)
                  Watch it, will you.

Phyllis slowly drops her hand from his arm. Both look up
as Dietrichson goes across the balcony and out of sight.

NEFF: Listen. That trip to Palo Alto
           When does he go?

PHYLLIS: End of the month.

NEFF: He drives, huh?

PHYLLIS: He always drives.

NEFF: Not this time. You're going to make
           him take the train.

PHYLLIS: Why?

NEFF: Because it's all worked out for a
           train.

For a second they stand listening and looking up as if
they had heard a sound.

PHYLLIS: It's all right. Go on, Walter.

NEFF: Look, baby. There's a clause in every
           accident policy, a little something
           called double indemnity. The insurance
           companies put it in as a sort of come-on
           for the customers. It means they pay
           double on certain accidents. The kind
           that almost never happen. Like for instance
           if a guy got killed on a train, they'd pay
           a hundred thousand instead of fifty.

9-30-43   (Continued)

B-3   (Cont'd)

PHYLLIS: I see.
                         (Her eyes widen with
                         excitement)

NEFF: We're hitting it for the limit, baby.
                  That's why it's got to be a train.

PHYLLIS: It's going to be a train, Walter.
                  Just the way you say. Straight down
                  the line.

They look at each other. The look is like a long kiss.
Neff goes out. Slowly Phyllis closes the door and leans
her head against it as she looks up the empty stairway.

B-4   <u>EXT. DIETRICHSON RESIDENCE</u> - (NIGHT)

Neff, briefcase under his arm, comes down the steps to the
street, where his Dodge coupe is parked at the curb. He
opens the door and stops, looking in.

Sitting there in the dark corner of the car, away from the
steering wheel, is Lola. She wears a coat but no hat.

LOLA: Hello, Mr. Neff. It's me.

Lola gives him a sly smile. Neff is a little annoyed.

NEFF: Something the matter?

LOLA: I've been waiting for you.

NEFF: For me? What for?

LOLA: I thought you could let me ride
                  with you, if you're going my way.

Neff doesn't like the idea very much.

NEFF: Which way would that be?

LOLA: Down the hill. Down Vermont.

NEFF: Oh, sure. Vermont and Franklin. North-west
(Remembering) corner, wasn't it?
                  Be glad to, Miss Dietrichson.

Neff gets into the car.

B-5   <u>INT. COUPE</u> - (NIGHT) - (TRANSPARENCY)

Neff puts the briefcase on the ledge behind the driver's
seat. He closes the door and starts the car. They drift
down the hill.

B-5   (Cont'd)

NEFF: Roller skating, eh? You like
                roller skating?

LOLA: I can take it or leave it.

Neff looks at her curiously. Lola meets his glance.

NEFF: Only tonight you're leaving it?

This is an embarrassing moment for Lola.

LOLA: Yes, I am. You see, Mr. Neff, I'm
                having a very tough time at home.
                My father doesn't understand me and
                Phyllis hates me.

NEFF: That does sound tough, all right.

LOLA: That's why I have to lie sometimes.

NEFF: You mean it's not Vermont and Franklin.

LOLA: It's Vermont and Franklin all right.
                Only it's not Anne Matthews. It's Nino
                Zacetti. You won't tell on me, will you?

NEFF: I'd have to think it over.

LOLA: Nino's not what my father says at all.
                He just had bad luck. He was doing
                pre-med at U.S.C. and working nights
                as an usher in a theater downtown. He
                got behind in his credits and flunked
                out. Then he lost his job for talking
                back. He's so hot-headed.

NEFF: That comes expensive, doesn't it?

LOLA: I guess my father thinks nobody's
                good enough for his daughter except
                maybe the guy that owns Standard Oil.
                Would you like a stick of gum?

NEFF: Never use it, thanks.

Lola puts a stick of gum in her mouth.

LOLA: I can't give Nino up. I wish father
                could see it my way.

NEFF: It'll straighten out all right,
                Miss Dietrichson.

9-30-43   (Continued)

B-5   (Cont'd)

     LOLA: I suppose it will sometime.
                       (Looking out)
                  This is the corner right here, Mr. Neff.

Neff brings the car to a stop by the curb.

     LOLA: There he is. By the bus stop.

Neff looks out.

B-6   CORNER VERMONT AND FRANKLIN - (NIGHT)

Zacchetti stands waiting, hands in trouser pockets. He is
about twenty-five, Italian looking, open shirt, not well
dressed.

B-7   <u>INT. COUPE</u> - (NIGHT) - LOLA AND NEFF

     IOLA: He needs a hair-cut, doesn't he.
                  Look at him. No job, no car, no
                  money, no prospects, no nothing.
                       (Pause)
                  I love him.

She leans over and honks on the horn.

     LOLA: (Calling)
                  Nino!

B-8   ZACCHETTI

He turns around and looks towards the car.

     LOLA'S   Over here, Nino.
     VOICE:

Zacchetti walks towards the car.

B-9   THE COUPE

Neff and Lola. She has opened the door. Zacchetti comes up.

     LOLA: This is Mr. Neff, Nino.

     NEFF: Hello, Nino.

     ZACCHETTI: (Belligerent from the
                      first word)
                  The name is Zacchetti.

     LOLA: Nino. Please. Mr. Neff gave me a
                  ride from the house. I told him all
                  about us.

9-30-43   (Continued)

ZACCHETTI: Why does he have to get told about us?

LOLA: We don't have to worry about Mr. Neff,
               Nino.

ZACCHETTI: I'm not doing any worrying. Just
               don't you broadcast so much.

LOLA: What's the matter with you, Nino?
               He's a friend.

ZACCHETTI: I don't have any friends. And if I
               did, I like to pick them myself.

NEFF: Look, sonny, she needed the ride and I
               brought her along. Is that anything
               to get tough about?

ZACCHETTI: All right, Lola, make up your mind.
               Are you coming or aren't you?

LOLA: Of course I'm coming. Don't mind him,
               Mr. Neff.

Lola steps out of the car.

LOLA: Thanks a lot. You've been very sweet.

Lola catches up with Zacchetti and they walk away together.

B-10   <u>INT. COUPE</u>

Neff looks after them.   NEFF'S VOICE
Slowly he puts the car in   She was a nice kid and maybe
gear and drives on. His   he was a little better than
face is tight. Behind   he sounded, I kind of hoped
his head, light catches   so for her sake, but right
the metal of the zipper   then it gave me a nasty feel-
on the briefcase. Over   ing to be thinking about them
the shot comes the   at all, with that briefcase
COMMENTARY: right behind my head and her
                              father's application in it.
                              Besides, I had other problems
                              to work out. There were plans
                              to make, and Phyllis had to
                              be in on them . . .

DISSOLVE TO:

B-11 EXT. SUPER MARKET - (DAY)

There is a fair amount of
activity but the place is
not crowded. Neff comes
along the sidewalk into the
shot. He passes in front
of the fruit and vegetable
display and goes between
the stalls into the market.

           NEFF'S VOICE
           (continued)
     . . . but we couldn't be seen

     together any more and I had

     told her never to call me

     from her house and never to

     call me at my office. So we

B-12 INT. MARKET

Neff stops by the cashier's
desk and buys a pack of
cigarettes. As he is opening the pack he looks back
casually beyond the turn-
stile into the rear part
of the market.

     had picked out a big market

     on Los Feliz. She was to be

     there buying stuff every day

     about eleven o'clock, and I

     could run into her there.

     Kind of accidentally on

     purpose.

B-13 ROWS OF HIGH SHELVES IN MARKET

The shelves are loaded with canned goods and other merchandise. Customers move around selecting articles and putting
them in their baskets. Phyllis is seen among them, standing
by the soap section. Her basket is partly filled. She
wears a simple house dress, no hat, and has a large envelope
pocketbook under her arm.

B-14 INT. MARKET

Neff has spotted Phyllis. Without haste he passes through
the turnstile towards the back.

B-15 THE SHELVES

Phyllis is putting a can of cleaning powder into her basket.
Neff enters the shot and moves along the shelves towards
her, very slowly, pretending to inspect the goods. A
customer passes and goes on out of scene. Phyllis and Neff
are now very close. During the ensuing low-spoken dialogue,
they continue to face the shelves, not looking at each other.

PHYLLIS: Walter.

NEFF: Not so loud.

PHYLLIS: I wanted to talk to you, Walter.
      Ever since yesterday.

11-27-43   (continued)

B-15 (Cont'd)

NEFF: Let me talk first. It's all set.
The accident policy came through. I've
got it in my pocket. I got his check
too. I saw him down in the oil fields.
He thought he was paying for the auto
insurance. The check's just made out
to the company. It could be for anything. But you have to send a check
for the auto insurance, see. It's all
right that way, because one of the cars
is yours.

PHYLLIS: But listen, Walter ---

NEFF: Quick, open your bag.

She hesitates, then opens it. Neff looks around quickly,
slips the policy out of his pocket and drops it into her
bag. She snaps the bag shut.

NEFF: Can you get into his safe deposit box?

PHYLLIS: Yes. We both have keys.

NEFF: Fine. But don't put the policy in
there yet. I'll tell you when. And
listen, you never touched it or even
saw it, understand?

PHYLLIS: I'm not a fool.

NEFF: Okay. When is he taking the train?

PHYLLIS: Walter, that's just it. He isn't going.

NEFF: What?

PHYLLIS: That's what I've been trying to tell
you. The trip is off.

NEFF: What's happened?

He breaks off as a short, squatty woman, pushing a child in
a walker, comes into sight and approaches. She stops beside
Neff, who is pretending to read a label on a can. Phyllis
puts a few cakes of soap into her basket.

WOMAN: (To Neff)
Mister, could you reach me that can of
coffee?
          (She points)
That one up there.

                                 (Continued)

B-15   (Cont'd)

NEFF: (Reaching up)
            This one?

She nods. Neff reaches a can down from the high shelf and hands
it to her.

WOMAN: I don't see why they always have to put
            what I want on the top shelf.

She moves away with her coffee and her child. Out of the
corner of his eye Neff watches her go. He moves closer to
Phyllis again.

NEFF: Go ahead. I'm listening.

PHYLLIS: He had a fall down at the well. He broke
            his leg. It's in a cast.

NEFF: That knocks it on the head all right.

PHYLLIS: What do we do, Walter?

NEFF: Nothing. Just wait.

PHYLLIS: Wait for what?

NEFF: Until he can take a train. I told
            you it's got to be a train.

PHYLLIS: We can't wait. I can't go on like this.

NEFF: We're not going to grab a hammer
            and do it quick, just to get it over
            with.

PHYLLIS: There are other ways.

NEFF: Only we're not going to do it other
            ways.

PHYLLIS: But we can't leave it like this. What
            do you think would happen if he found
            out about this accident policy?

NEFF: Plenty. But not as bad as sitting
            in that death-house.

PHYLLIS: Don't ever talk like that, Walter.

NEFF: Just don't let's start losing our heads.

B-15 (Cont'd)

    PHYLLIS: It's not our heads. It's our nerve
                      we're losing.

    NEFF: We're going to do it right. That's
                      all I said.

    PHYLLIS: Walter maybe it's my nerves. It's
                      the waiting that gets me.

    NEFF: It's getting me just as bad, baby.
                      But we've got to wait.

    PHYLLIS: Maybe we have, Walter. Only it's so
                      tough without you. It's like a wall
                      between us.

Neff looks at his watch.

    NEFF: Good-bye baby. I'm thinking of
                      you every minute.

He goes off. She stares after him.

DISSOLVE TO:

B-16   <u>NEFF'S OFFICE</u> - (DAY)

	NEFF'S VOICE
He is wearing a light grey suit and has his hat on. He is standing behind his desk opening some mail, taking a few papers out of his brief-case, checking something in his rate book, making a quick telephone call. But nothing of this is heard.	After that a full week went by and I didn't see her once. I tried to keep my mind off her and off the whole idea. I kept telling myself that maybe those fates they say watch over you had gotten together and broken his leg to give me a way out. Then it was the fifteenth of June. You may remember that date, Keyes. I do too, only for a **very different** reason. You came into my office around three in the afternoon...

Keyes enters with some papers in his hand.

NEFF: Hello, Keyes.

KEYES: I just came from Norton's office. The semi-annual sales records are out. You're high man, Walter. That's twice in a row. Congratulations.

NEFF: Thanks. How would you like a cheap drink?

KEYES: How would you like a fifty dollar cut in salary?

NEFF: How would I -- Do I laugh now, or wait until it gets funny?

KEYES: I'm serious, Walter. I've been talking to Norton. There's too much stuff piling up on my desk. Too much pressure on my nerves. I spend half the night walking up and down in my bed. I've got to have an assistant. I thought that you --

NEFF: Me? Why pick on me?

KEYES: Because I've got a crazy idea you might be good at the job.

NEFF: That's crazy all right. I'm a salesman.

KEYES: Yeah. A peddler, a glad-hander, a back-slapper. You're too good to be a salesman.

NEFF: Nobody's too good to be a salesman.

10-2-43   (Continued)

B-16 (Cont'd)

KEYES: Phooey. All you guys do is ring door-
bells and dish out a smooth line of
monkey talk. What's bothering you is
that fifty buck cut, isn't it?

NEFF: That'd bother anybody.

KEYES: Look, Walter. The job I'm talking
about takes brains and integrity. It
takes more guts than there is in fifty
salesmen. It's the hottest job in the
business.

NEFF: It's still a desk job. I don't want
a desk job.

KEYES: A desk job. Is that all you can see
in it? Just a hard chair to park
your pants on from nine to five. Just
a pile of papers to shuffle around,
and five sharp pencils and a scratch
pad to make figures on, with maybe a
little doodling on the side. That's
not the way I see it, Walter. To me
a claims man is a surgeon, and that
desk is an operating table, and those
pencils are scalpels and bone chisels.
And those papers are not just forms
and statistics and claims for compensation. They're alive, they're packed
with drama, with twisted hopes and
crooked dreams. A claims man, Walter,
is a doctor and a blood-hound and a
cop and a judge and a jury and a father
confessor, all in one.

The telephone rings on Neff's desk. Automatically Keyes
grabs the phone and answers.

KEYES: Who? Okay, hold the line.

He puts the phone down on the desk and continues to Neff:

KEYES: And you want to tell me you're not
interested. You don't want to work
with your brains. All you want to
work with is your finger on a doorbell. For a few bucks more a week.
There's a dame on your phone.

Neff picks the phone up and answers.

NEFF: Walter Neff speaking.

10-2-43

B-17   INT. PHONE BOOTH - MARKET

Phyllis is on the phone.

PHYLLIS: I had to call you, Walter. It's
                terribly urgent. Are you with
                somebody?

B-18   NEFF'S OFFICE

Neff on the phone. His eye catches Keyes', who is walking
up and down.

NEFF: Of course I am. Can't I call you
                back ... Margie?

B-19   PHYLLIS - ON PHONE

PHYLLIS: Walter, I've only got a minute.
                It can't wait. Listen. He's
                going tonight. On the train.
                Are you listening, Walter? Walter!

B-20   NEFF - ON PHONE

His eyes are on Keyes. He speaks into the phone as calmly
as possible.

NEFF: I'm listening. Only make it short...
                Margie.

B-21   PHYLLIS - ON PHONE

PHYLLIS: He's on crutches. The doctor says
                he can go if he's careful. The
                change will do him good. It's
                wonderful, Walter. Just the way
                you wanted it. Only with the crutches
                it's ever so much better, isn't it?

B-22   NEFF'S OFFICE

Neff on phone.

NEFF: One hundred percent better. Hold
                the line a minute.

He covers the receiver with his hand and turns to Keyes,
who is now standing at the window.

NEFF: Suppose I join you in your office,
                Keyes --

                                        (Continued)

B-22   (cont'd)

He makes a gesture as if expecting Keyes to leave. Keyes stays right where he is.

KEYES: I'll wait. Only tell Margie not
              to take all day.

Neff looks at Keyes' back with a strained expression, then lifts the phone again.

NEFF: Go ahead.

B-23   PHYLLIS, <u>ON PHONE</u>

PHYLLIS: It's the ten-fifteen from Glendale.
              I'm driving him. Is it still that
              same dark street?

B-24   NEFF, <u>ON PHONE</u>

He is still watching Keyes cautiously.

NEFF: Yeah -- sure.

B-24a   CLOSEUP - PHYLLIS - <u>ON PHONE</u>

PHYLLIS: The signal is three honks on the
              horn. Is there anything else?

B-24b   CLOSEUP NEFF, <u>ON PHONE</u>

NEFF: What color did you pick out?

B-25   PHYLLIS, <u>ON PHONE</u>

PHYLLIS: Color?
                   (She catches on)
              Oh, sure. The blue suit, Walter.
              Navy blue. And the cast on his
              left leg.

B-26   NEFF, <u>ON PHONE</u>

NEFF: Navy blue. I like that fine.

B-27   PHYLLIS, <u>ON PHONE</u>

PHYLLIS: This is it, Walter. I'm shaking
              like a leaf. But it's straight
              down the line now for both of us.
              I love you, Walter. Goodbye.

B-28   <u>NEFF'S OFFICE</u>

Neff on the phone.

                                       (Continued)

B-28 (Cont'd)

NEFF: So long, Margie.

He hangs up. His mouth is grim, but he forces a smile as
Keyes turns.

NEFF: I'm sorry, Keyes.

KEYES: What's the matter? The dames
                    chasing you again? Or still?
                    Or is it none of my business?

NEFF: (With a sour smile)
                    If I told you it was a customer --

KEYES: Margie! I bet she drinks from the
                    bottle. Why don't you settle down
                    and get married, Walter?

NEFF: Why don't you, for instance?

KEYES: I almost did, once. A long time
                    ago.

Neff gets up from his desk.

NEFF: Look, Keyes, I've got a prospect
                    to call on.

Keyes drives right ahead.

KEYES: We even had the church all picked
                    out, the dame and I. She had a white
                    satin dress with flounces on it. And
                    I was on my way to the jewelry store
                    to buy the ring. Then suddenly that
                    little man in here started working on
                    me.

He punches his stomach with his fist.

NEFF: So you went back and started investi-
                    gating her. That it?

Keyes nods slowly, a little sad and a little ashamed.

KEYES: And the stuff that came out. She'd
                    been dyeing her hair ever since she
                    was sixteen. And there was a manic-
                    depressive in her family, on her
                    mother's side. And she already had
                    one husband, a professional pool
                    player in Baltimore. And as for her
                    brother --

NEFF: I get the general idea. She was a
                    tramp from a long line of tramps.
                                              (Continued)

57

He picks up some papers impatiently.

KEYES: All right, I'm going. What am I to
               say to Norton? How about that job I
               want you for?

NEFF: I don't think I want it. Thanks,
               Keyes, just the same.

KEYES: Fair enough. Just get this: I
               picked you for the job, not because I
               think you're so darn smart, but because
               I thought maybe you were a shade less
               dumb than the rest of the outfit. I
               guess I was all wet. You're not smarter,
               Walter. You're just a little taller.

He goes out. Neff is alone.   NEFF'S VOICE
He watches the door close,   That was it, Keyes, and there
then turns and goes slowly   was no use kidding myself any
to the water cooler. He   more. Those fates I was talk-
fills a paper cup and   ing about had only been stall-
stands holding it. His   ing me off. Now they had
thoughts are somewhere else.   thrown the switch. The gears
After a moment he absently   had meshed. The machinery had
throws the cupful of water   started to move and nothing
into the receptacle under   could stop it. The time for
the cooler. He goes back   thinking had all run out. From
to the desk. . . . .   here on it was a question of
He takes his rate book out   following the time table, move
of his brief case and puts   by move, just as we had it re-
it on the desk. He buttons   hearsed. I wanted my time all
the top button of his shirt,   accounted for for the rest of
and pulls his tie right. He   the afternoon and up to the
leaves the office, with his   last possible moment in the
briefcase under his arm.   evening. So I arranged to call
                                   on a prospect in Pasadena about
                                   a public liability bond. When
                                   I left the office I put my rate
                                   book on the desk as if I had
                                   forgotten it. That was part of
                                   the alibi.

       DISSOLVE TO:

B-29   <u>EXT. NEFF'S APT. HOUSE</u>   NEFF'S VOICE
       <u>DAY</u>   I got home about seven and
                                   drove right into the garage.
Neff's coupe comes down   This was another item to es-
the street and swings   tablish my alibi.
into the garage and goes
down the ramp into the
basement.

B-30   <u>INT. GARAGE</u>

There are about eight cars parked. A colored attendant in coveralls and rubber boots is washing a car with a hose and sponge. Neff's car comes into the shot and stops near the attendant. Neff gets out with his briefcase under his arm.

ATTENDANT: Hiya there, Mr. Neff.

NEFF: How about a wash job on my heap,
                Charlie?

ATTENDANT: How soon you want it, Mr. Neff?
                I got two cars ahead of you.

NEFF: Anytime you get to it, Charlie.
                I'm staying in tonight.

ATTENDANT: Okay, Mr. Neff. Be all shined up
                for you in the morning.

Neff is crossing to the elevator. He speaks back over his shoulder:

NEFF: That left front tire looks a little
                soft. Check it, will you?

ATTENDANT: You bet. Check 'em all round.
                Always do.

Neff enters the elevator.

DISSOLVE TO:

B-31   <u>NEFF'S APT. - (DAY)</u>

Neff enters. He walks straight to the phone, dials, and starts speaking into the mouthpiece, but only the COMMENTARY is heard.

DISSOLVE:

NEFF'S VOICE

Up in my apartment I called Lou Schwartz, one of the salesmen that shared my office. He lived in Westwood. That made it a toll call and there'd be a record of it. I told him I had forgotten my rate book and needed some dope on the public liability bond I was figuring. I asked him to call me back. This was another item in my alibi, so that later on I could prove that I had been home.

B-32   <u>INT. NEFF'S LIVING ROOM</u>

Neff comes into the living room from the bedroom, putting on the jacket of his blue suit. THE PHONE RINGS. He picks up the receiver and starts talking, unheard, as before. He makes notes on a pad.

DISSOLVE TO:

NEFF'S VOICE

I changed into a navy blue suit like Dietrichson was going to wear. Lou Schwartz called me back and gave me a lot of figures. . . . . . .

I stuffed a hand towel

and a big roll of adhesive

B-33 NEFF   tape into my pockets, so

He is folding a hand towel   I could fake something that
and stuffing it into his
jacket pocket. He then   looked like a cast on a
takes a large roll of ad-
hesive tape and puts that   broken leg. . . Next I
into his pants pocket.
                                  fixed the telephone and the
DISSOLVE TO:
                                  doorbell, so that the cards
B-34 INSERTS OF OPEN TELEPHONE
&   BELL BOX (ON BASEBOARD) &   would fall down if the bells
B-35 DOORBELL (ABOVE ENTRANCE
      DOOR)   rang. That way I would know

Neff's hand places a small   there had been a phone call
card against the bell
clapper in each of these.   or visitor while I was away.

DISSOLVE TO: I left the apartment house

B-36 FIRE STAIRS, APT. HOUSE   by the fire stairs and side
      (NIGHT)
                                  door. Nobody saw me. It
CAMERA PANS with Neff go-
ing down the stairs in his   was already getting dark.
blue suit, with a hat
pulled down over his eyes.   I took the Vermont Avenue

DISSOLVE TO: bus to Los Feliz and walked

B-37 EXT. DIETRICHSON HOME -   from there up to the Dietrichson
      (NIGHT) - LONG SHOT -
      NO TRAFFIC   house. There was that smell

Some windows are lit. Neff   of honeysuckle again, only
comes into the shot and
approaches cautiously. He   stronger, now that it was
looks around and then
slides open the garage door.   evening.

                                          NEFF'S VOICE
B-38 INT. GARAGE
                                  Then I was in the garage.
Neff closes the garage door.
Very faint light comes in at   His car was backed in, just
a side window. He opens the
rear door of the sedan, gets   the way I told Phyllis to
in and closes the door after
him. The dark interior of   have it. It was so still
the car has swallowed him
up.

B-38   (Cont'd)

                                          NEFF'S VOICE (Cont'd)
I could hear the ticking of the clock on the dashboard. I kept thinking of the place we had picked out to do it, that dark street on the way to the station, and the three honks on

B-39   EXT. DIETRICHSON HOUSE   the horn that were to be the

The front door has opened   signal ... About ten minutes
and Dietrichson is half-
way down the steps. He is   later they came down.
walking with crutches, wear-
ing the dark blue suit and a
hat. The cast is on his
left leg. There is no shoe
on his left foot. Only the
white plaster shows. Phyllis
comes after him, carrying his
suitcase and his overcoat. She
wears a camel's-hair coat and
no hat. She catches up with him.

PHYLLIS: You all right, honey? I'll have
              the car out in a second.

Dietrichson just grunts. She passes him to the garage,
CAMERA WITH HER, and slides the door open.

B-40   INT. GARAGE

THE CAMERA IS VERY LOW INSIDE THE SEDAN, shooting slightly
upwards from Neff's hiding place. The garage door has just
been opened. Phyllis comes to the car, opens the rear door.
She looks down, almost INTO THE CAMERA. A tight, cool smile
flashes across her face. Then, very calmly, she puts the
suitcase and overcoat in back on the seat (out of shot). She
closes the door again.

B-41   EXT. GARAGE

Dietrichson stands watching Phyllis as she gets into the car
and drives out to pick him up. She stops beside him and
opens the right-hand door. Dietrichson climbs in with difficulty. She helps him, watching him closely.

PHYLLIS: Take it easy, honey. We've got
              lots of time.

                                         (Continued)

B-41 (Cont'd)

DIETRICHSON: Just let me do it my own way.
                       Grab that crutch.

She takes one of the crutches from him.

DIETRICHSON: They ought to make these things so
                       they fold up.

For a moment, as he leans his hand on the back of the seat,
there is danger that he may see Neff. He doesn't. He
slides awkwardly into the seat and pulls the second crutch
in after him. He closes the door. The car moves off.

DISSOLVE TO:

B-42 INT. CAR

Phyllis driving and Dietrichson beside her, face TOWARDS THE
CAMERA. Dietrichson has a partly smoked cigar between his
teeth. They are in the middle of a conversation.

DIETRICHSON: Aw, stop squawkin' can't you, Phyllis?
                       No man takes his wife along to a class
                       reunion. That's what class reunions
                       are for.

PHYLLIS: Mrs. Tucker went along with her husband
                       last year, didn't she.

DIETRICHSON: Yeah, and what happened to her? She sat
                       in the hotel lobby for four days straight.
                       Never even saw the guy until we poured
                       him back on the train.

B-43 CLOSEUP ON NEFF'S FACE LOW DOWN IN THE CORNER BEHIND
DIETRICHSON

His face is partly covered by the edge of a traveling rug
which he has pulled up over him. He looks up at Dietrichson
and Phyllis in the front seat.

PHYLLIS   All right, honey. Just so long as you
VOICE: have a good time.

DIETRICHSON'S   I won't do much dancing, I can tell
VOICE: you that.

B-44 HEADS & SHOULDERS OF DIETRICHSON & PHYLLIS - AS SEEN BY NEFF

PHYLLIS: Remember what the doctor said. If
                       you get careless you might end up
                       with a shorter leg.

10-2-43   (Continued)

B-44 (Cont'd)

    DIETRICHSON: So what? I could break the
                    other one and match them up again.

    PHYLLIS: It makes you feel pretty good to get
                    away from me, doesn't it?

B-45 PHYLLIS & DIETRICHSON - FACING CAMERA

    DIETRICHSON: It's only for four days. I'll be back
                    Monday at the latest.

    PHYLLIS: Don't forget we're having the Hobeys
                    for dinner on Monday.

    DIETRICHSON: The Hobeys? We had them last. They
                    owe us a dinner, don't they?

    PHYLLIS: Maybe they do but I've already asked
                    them for Monday.

    DIETRICHSON: Well, I don't want to feed the Hobeys.

B-46 CLOSEUP - PHYLLIS' FACE ONLY

There is a look of tension in her eyes now. She glances
around quickly. The car has reached the dark street Neff
and she picked out.

    DIETRICHSON'S   And I don't want to eat at their house
    VOICE: either. The food you get there, and
                    that rope he hands out for cigars. Call
                    if off, can't you?

Phyllis does not answer. She doesn't even breathe. Her hand
goes down on the horn button. She honks three times.

    DIETRICHSON'S   What are you doing that for? What the --
    VOICE:

This is as far as his voice will ever get. It breaks off and
dies down in a muffled groan. There are struggling noises
and a dull sound of something breaking. Phyllis drives on
and never turns her head. She stares straight in front of
her. Her teeth are clenched.

    DISSOLVE TO:

B-47 PARKING SPACE ADJOINING GLENDALE STATION - NIGHT

The station is visible about sixty yards away. There is no
parking attendant. Ten or twelve cars are parked diagonally,
not crowded. The train is not in yet, but there is activity
around the station. Passengers and their friends, redcaps
and baggage men, news vendors, etc.

10-2-43   (Continued)

B-47 (Cont'd)

The Dietrichson sedan drives into the shot past CAMERA and parks in the foreground at the outer end of the line, several spaces from the next car, facing away from the CAMERA. Both front doors are open. Phyllis gets out and from the other side crutches emerge, and a man (seen entirely from behind, and apparently Dietrichson) climbs out awkwardly. While he is steadying himself on the ground with the crutches, Phyllis has taken out Dietrichson's suitcase and overcoat. She walks around the car and rolls up the right front window. She closes and locks the car door. She tries the right rear door and takes a last look into the dim interior of the car. Then she and the man walk slowly away from the car to the end of the station platform and along it toward the station building. Phyllis walks several steps ahead of the man.

B-48   PHYLLIS & THE MAN - WALKING

CAMERA FOLLOWING THEM, a little to one side, so that Phyllis is clearly seen but the man's face is not.

MAN: (In a subdued voice)
                   You handle the redcap and the conductor.

PHYLLIS: Don't worry.

MAN: Keep them away from me as much as you
               can. I don't want to be helped.

PHYLLIS: I said don't worry, Walter.

B-49   PHYLLIS & THE MAN, WALKING <u>DOWN PLATFORM</u>, CAMERA NOW PRECEDING THEM

Only at this point is it quite clear that THE MAN IS NEFF

NEFF: You start just as soon as the train
               leaves. At the dairy sign you turn
               off the highway onto the dirt road.
               From there it's exactly eight-tenths
               of a mile to the dump beside the
               tracks. Remember?

PHYLLIS: I remember everything.

NEFF: You'll be there a little ahead of the
               train. No speeding. You don't want
               any cops stopping you -- with him in
               the back.

PHYLLIS: Walter, we've been through all that
               so many times.

10-2-43   (Continued)

B-49 (Cont'd)

> NEFF: When you turn off the highway, cut
> all your lights. I'm going to be
> back on the observation platform.
> I'll drop off as close to the spot
> as I can. Wait for the train to pass,
> then blink your lights twice.

Phyllis nods. They go on. Over them is heard the noise of
the train coming into the station and its lights are seen.

B-50   <u>GLENDALE STATION PLATFORM</u>

The train is just coming to a stop. The passengers move forward to the tracks. Phyllis, carrying the suitcase and overcoat, and Neff, still a little behind her, come TOWARDS THE
CAMERA. A redcap sees them and runs up. He takes the suitcase out of Phyllis' hand.

> REDCAP: San Francisco train, lady?

Phyllis takes an envelope containing Dietrichson's ticket
from the pocket of the overcoat. She reads from the
envelope.

> PHYLLIS: Car nine, section eleven. Just
> my husband going.

> REDCAP: Car nine, section eleven. Yessum,
> this way please.

Phyllis hands the overcoat to the redcap, who leads her and
Neff towards car number nine. Neff still hangs back and
keeps his head down, the way a man using crutches might
naturally do.

B-51   <u>EXT. CAR #9</u>
B-52
B-53   The pullman conductor and porter stand at the steps. The
conductor is checking the tickets of passengers getting on.
The redcap leads Phyllis and **Neff into** the SHOT. The conductor and porter see Neff on his crutches and move to
help him.

> PHYLLIS: It's all right, thanks. My husband
> doesn't like to be helped.

The redcap goes up the steps into the car. Neff laboriously
swings himself up onto the box and from there up on the
steps, keeping his head down. Meantime, Phyllis is holding
the attention of the conductor and porter by showing them
the ticket.

> CONDUCTOR: Car nine, section eleven. The gentleman
> only. Thank you.

Phyllis nods and takes the ticket back. Neff has reached the
top of the steps. She goes up after him and gives him the
ticket. They are now close together.
                               (Continued)

B-51 (Cont'd)
B-52
B-53 PHYLLIS: Goodbye, honey. Take awful good
                   care of yourself with that leg.

     NEFF: Sure, I will. Just you take it
                   easy going home.

     PHYLLIS: I'll miss you, honey.

She kisses him. There are shouts of "ALL ABOARD". The redcap comes from inside the car.

     REDCAP: Section eleven, suh.

Phyllis takes a quarter from her bag and gives it to the
redcap.

     PORTER: (Shouting)
                   All aboard!

Redcap descends. Phyllis kisses Neff again quickly.

     PHYLLIS: Good luck, honey.

She runs down the steps. The porter picks up the box. He
and the conductor get on board the train. Phyllis stands
there waving goodbye as the train starts moving, and the
porter begins to close the car door. Phyllis turns and
walks out of the shot in the direction of the parked car.

B-54 INT. PLATFORM CAR NUMBER NINE - MOVING TRAIN - (NIGHT) -
     DIM LIGHT

Neff and the Porter. The conductor is going on into the car.
Neff is half turned away from the porter.

     NEFF: Can you make up my berth right
                   away?

     PORTER: Yes, sir.

     NEFF: I'm going back to the observation
                   car for a smoke.

     PORTER: This way, sir. Three cars back.

He holds the vestibule door open. Neff hobbles through.

     DISSOLVE TO:

B-55 INT. PULLMAN CAR - DIM

Most of the berths are made up. As Neff hobbles along,
another porter and some passengers make way for the crippled
man solicitously.

     DISSOLVE TO:
                                        (more)

B-56   PLATFORM BETWEEN TWO CARS - VERY DIM

The train conductor meets Neff and opens the door for him.
Neff hobbles on through.

DISSOLVE TO:

B-57   INT. PARLOR CAR - MOVING TRAIN

Four or five passengers are reading or writing. As Neff
comes through on his crutches they pull in their feet to
make room for him. One old lady, seeing that he is headed
for the observation platform, opens the door for him. He
thanks her with a nod and hobbles through.

B-58   OBSERVATION PLATFORM

Dark except for a little light coming from inside the parlor
car. The train is going at about fifteen miles an hour between Glendale and Burbank. Neff has come out and hobbled
to the railing. He stands looking back along the rails.
SUDDENLY A MAN'S VOICE speaks from behind him.

MAN'S VOICE: Can I pull a chair out for you?

Neff looks around. He sees a man sitting in the corner
smoking a hand-rolled cigarette. He is about fifty-five
years old, with white hair, and a broad-brimmed Stetson
hat. He looks like a small town lawyer or maybe a mining
man. Neff does not like the man's presence there very much.
He turns to him just enough to answer.

NEFF: No thanks, I'd rather stand.

MAN: You going far?

NEFF: Palo Alto.

MAN :   My name's Jackson. I'm going all the
                    way to Medford. Medford, Oregon. Had
                    a broken arm myself once.

NEFF: Uh-huh.

JACKSON: That darn cast sure itches something
                    fierce, don't it? I thought I'd go
                    crazy with mine.

Neff stands silent. His mind is feverishly thinking of
how to get rid of Jackson.

JACKSON: Palo Alto's a nice little town. You a
                    Stanford man?

NEFF: Used to be.

He starts patting his pockets as if looking for something.

JACKSON: I bet you left something behind. I
                     always do.

NEFF: My cigar case. Must have left it in my
                     overcoat back in the section.

Jackson takes out a small bag of tobacco and a packet of
cigarette papers.

JACKSON: Care to roll yourself a cigarette,
                     Mr. --- ?

NEFF: Dietrichson. Thanks. I really prefer
                     cigars.
                              (Looking around)
                     Maybe the porter ---

JACKSON: I could get your cigars for you. Be
                     glad to, Mr. Dietrichson.

NEFF: That's darn nice of you. It's car
                     nine, section eleven. If you're sure
                     it's not too much trouble.

JACKSON: Car nine, section eleven. A pleasure.

He rises and exits into the parlor car. Neff turns slowly
and watches Jackson go back through the car. Then he moves
to one side of the platform and looks ahead along the track
to orientate himself. He gives one last glance back into
the parlor car to make sure no one is watching him. He
slips the crutches from under his arms and stands on both
feet. He drops the crutches off the train onto the tracks,
then quickly swings his body over the rail.

B-59 EXT. MOVING OBSERVATION CAR - CAMERA FOLLOWING

Neff is hanging onto the railing. He looks down, then lets
go and drops to the right-of-way. THE CAMERA STOPS. The
train recedes slowly into the night. Neff has fallen on
the tracks. He picks himself up, rubs one knee and looks
back along the line of the tracks and off to one side.

B-60 DARK LANDSCAPE - RAILROAD TRACKS

Close beyond the edge of the right-of-way, the silhouette of
a dump shows up. Beside it looms the dark bulk of the
Dietrichson sedan. The headlights blink twice and go out.

10-2-43

B-61 NEFF

> He starts running towards the car. He runs a little awkward-
> ly because of the improvised cast on his left foot.

B-62 <u>CAR IN THE DARK</u>

> The front door opens and Phyllis steps out. She closes the
> door and looks in the direction of the tracks. The uneven
> steps of Neff running towards her are heard. She opens the
> back door of the car and leans in. She pulls the rug off
> the corpse (which is not visible) and stands looking into
> the car, unable to take her eyes off what she sees, while
> at the same time her hands mechanically begin to fold the
> rug. The running steps grow louder and Neff comes into the
> SHOT breathing hard. He reaches her.

> NEFF: Okay. This has to go fast. Take
>   his hat and pick up the crutches.

> Neff points back towards the tracks. He reaches into the
> car and begins to drag out the body by the armpits. Phyllis
> coolly reaches past him and takes the hat off the dead man's
> head. She turns to go.

> NEFF: Hang on to that rug. I'll need it.

> Phyllis moves out of the shot carrying the hat and rug.

B-63 NEFF

> He gets a stronger hold on the dead Dietrichson and drags
> him free of the car and towards the tracks. The corpse is
> not seen.

B-64 PHYLLIS

> She has reached the point where one of the crutches lies.
> She picks it up and goes for the other crutch a short dis-
> tance away. She carries both crutches, the hat and the rug
> towards Neff.

B-65 NEFF

> He has reached the railroad tracks. The corpse is lying be-
> side the tracks, face down. Phyllis comes up to Neff. He
> takes the crutches and the hat from her. He throws the
> crutches beside the corpse. He takes the hat from Phyllis
> and tosses it carelessly along the track.

> NEFF: Let's go. Stay behind me.

10-2-43   (Continued)

B-65 (Cont'd)

He takes the rug from her and they move back towards the car,
Phyllis first, then Neff walking almost backwards, sweeping
the ground over which the body was dragged with the rug as
they go.

B-66 <u>THE CAR</u>

They reach it together.

NEFF: Get in. You drive.

She gets in. Neff sweeps the ground after him as he goes
around the car to get in beside her. He throws the rug into
the back of the car.

B-67 <u>INT. CAR</u>

Phyllis is behind the wheel. Neff beside her is just closing
the door. He props his wrapped foot against the dashboard
and begins to tear off the adhesive tape while at the same
time Phyllis presses the starter button. The starter grinds,
but the motor doesn't catch. She tries again. It still
doesn't catch. Neff looks at her. She tries a third time.
The starter barely turns over. The battery is very low.

Phyllis leans back. They stare at each other desperately.
After a moment Neff bends forward slowly and turns the ignition key to the OFF position. He holds his left thumb
poised over the starter button. There is a breathless moment.
Then he presses the starter button with swift decision. The
starter grinds with nerve-wracking sluggishness. Neff twists
the ignition key to ON and instantly pulls the hand-throttle
wide open. With a last feeble kick of the starter, the motor
catches and races. He eases the throttle down and slides
back into his place. They look at each other again. The
tenseness of the moment still shows in their faces.

NEFF: Let's go, baby.

Phyllis releases the hand brake and puts the car in reverse.
Neff is again busy unwrapping the tape from his leg. The
car moves.

B-68 <u>DARK LANDSCAPE - WITH DUMP</u>

The car, with the headlights out, backs up, swings around and
moves off along the dirt road the way it came.

DISSOLVE TO:

10-2-43

B-69   INT. SEDAN - DRIVING ALONG
       HIGHWAY IN TRAFFIC

Phyllis and Neff facing to-   NEFF'S VOICE
wards CAMERA. Neff is bent   On the way back we went over
over, peeling the towel and
plaster off his foot, which   once more what she was to do at
is out of shot. Phyllis is
calm, almost relaxed. Neff   the inquest, if they had one,
straightens up. They are
talking to each other.   and about the insurance, when
Their lips are seen moving
but what they say is not   that came up.
heard.

                          I was afraid she might go to
They stop talking. Phyllis
stares straight ahead. Neff pieces a little, now that we
is pulling adhesive tape off
the wrapped towel that was   had done it, but she was
on his foot. He folds the
adhesive into a tight ball, perfect. No nerves. Not a
rolls the towel up, puts
both into his pockets.   tear, not even a blink of the

DISSOLVE TO: eyes....

B-70   DARK STREET NEAR NEFF'S
       APT. HOUSE

The sedan drives into the   She dropped me a block from
shot and stops without
pulling over to the curb.   my apartment house.

The car door opens. Neff starts to get out.

PHYLLIS: Walter.

Neff turns back to her.

PHYLLIS: What's the matter, Walter. Aren't
                you going to kiss me?

NEFF: Sure, I'm going to kiss you.

Phyllis bends towards him and puts her arms around him.

PHYLLIS: It's straight down the line, isn't it?

Phyllis kisses him. In the kiss he is passive.

PHYLLIS: I love you, Walter.

NEFF: I love you, baby.

DISSOLVE TO:

B-71 FIRE STAIRS - (NIGHT)   NEFF'S VOICE

      Neff going up.   It was two minutes past eleven

                                          as I went up the fire stairs

                                          again. Nobody saw me this time

                                          either.

      DISSOLVE TO:

B-72 INSERTS
B-73
      Telephone bell box and the   In the apartment I checked the
      door bell. The cards are
      still in position. Neff's   bells. The cards hadn't moved
      hand takes them out.
                                          No calls. No visitors.

      DISSOLVE TO:

B-74 LIVING ROOM - NEFF'S APT.
      NIGHT - ELECTRIC LIGHTS ON

      Neff comes from the bedroom,   I changed the blue suit.
      wearing the light grey suit
      he wore before the murder,   There was one last thing to
      only without a tie. He but-
      tons his jacket, looks   do. I wanted the garage man
      around the room, and opens
      the corridor door.   to see me again.

      DISSOLVE TO:

B-75 BASEMENT GARAGE - (NIGHT)

      Fifteen or twenty cars are parked now. Charlie, the attendant
      has washed Neff's car and is now polishing the glass and metal
      work. Neff comes from the elevator. Charlie sees him. He
      straightens up.

          CHARLIE: You going to need it after all,
                         Mr. Neff? I'm about through.

          NEFF: It's okay, Charlie. Just walking down
                         to the drug store for something to eat.
                         Been working upstairs all evening. My
                         stomach's getting sore at me.

      He walks up the ramp towards the garage entrance.

10-4-43

B-76 STREET OUTSIDE APT. HOUSE –
      (NIGHT) – SHOOTING TOWARDS
      GARAGE ENTRANCE   NEFF'S VOICE

Neff comes out at the top of   That was all there was to it.
the ramp and starts to walk
down the street, not too   Nothing had slipped, nothing
fast. CAMERA PRECEDES HIM.
He walks about ten or fif-   had been overlooked, there
teen yards. At first his
steps sound hard and dis-   was nothing to give us away.
tinct on the sidwalk and
echo in the deserted street.   And yet, Keyes, as I was walk-
But slowly, as he goes on,
they fade into utter sil-   ing down the street to the
ence. He walks a few feet
without sound, then becomes   drug store, suddenly it came
aware of the silence. He
stops rigidly and looks   over me that everything would
back. CAMERA STOPS WITH HIM.
He stands like that for a   go wrong. It sounds crazy,
moment, then turns toward
the CAMERA again. There is   Keyes, but it's true, so help
a look of horror on his face
now. He walks on, CAMERA   me: I couldn't hear my own
AHEAD OF HIM again. Still his
steps make no sound.   footsteps. It was the walk of

                                    a dead man.

FADE OUT:

                    END OF SEQUENCE "B"

73

FADE IN:

C-1   NEFF'S OFFICE - NIGHT

Neff sits before the dictaphone. There are four cylinders on end on the desk next to him. He gets up from the swivel chair with great effort and stands a moment unsteadily. The wound in his shoulder is paining him. He is very weak as he slowly crosses to the water coller. He takes the blood stained handkerchief from inside his shirt and soaks it with fresh water.

The office door opens behind him. He turns, hiding the handkerchief behind his back. In the doorway stands the colored man who has been cleaning up downstairs. He is carrying his big trash box by a rope handle.

COLORED MAN: Didn't know anybody was here, Mr. Neff. We ain't cleaned your office yet.

NEFF: Let it go tonight. I'm busy.

COLORED MAN: Whatever you say, Mr. Neff.

He closes the door slowly, staring at Neff with an uneasy expression. Neff puts the soaked handkerchief back on his wounded shoulder, then walks heavily over to his swivel chair and lowers himself into it. He takes the dictaphone horn and speaks into it again.

NEFF: That was the longest night I ever lived through, Keyes, and the next day was worse, when the story broke in the papers, and they were talking about it at the office, and the day after that when you started digging into it. I kept my hands in my pockets because I thought they were shaking, and I put on dark glasses so people couldn't see my eyes, and then I took them off again so people wouldn't get to wondering why I wore them. I was trying to hold myself together, but I could feel my nerves pulling me to pieces.....

DISSOLVE TO:

C-2   INSURANCE OFFICE - TWELFTH FLOOR - DAY

Neff comes through the reception room doors with his hat on and his briefcase under his arm. He walks towards his office, but half way there he runs into Keyes. Keyes is wearing his

10-4-43   (Continued)

C-2   (Cont'd)

vest and hat, no coat. He is carrying a file of papers and smoking a cigar.

KEYES: Come on, Walter. The big boss
                  wants to see us.

NEFF: Okay.

He turns and walks beside Keyes, CAMERA AHEAD of them

NEFF: That Dietrichson case?

KEYES: Must be.

NEFF: Anything wrong?

KEYES: The guy's dead, we had him insured
                  and it's going to cost us money.
                  That's always wrong.

He stops by a majolica jar full of sand and takes a pencil from his vest. He stands over the jar extinguishing his cigar carefully so as not to damage it.

NEFF: What have you got so far?

KEYES: Autopsy report. No heart failure,
                  no apoplexy, no predisposing medical
                  cause of any kind. He died of a
                  broken neck.

NEFF: When is the inquest?

KEYES: They had it this morning. His wife
                  and daughter made the identification.
                  The train people and some passengers
                  told how he went through to the
                  observation car..It was all over in
                  forty-five minutes. Verdict,
                  accidental death.

Keyes puts the half-smoked cigar into his vest pocket with the pencil. They move on.

NEFF: What do the police figure?

KEYES: That he got tangled up in his crutches
                  and fell off the train. They're satisfied.
                  It's not their dough.

They stop at a door lettered in embossed chromium letters: EDWARD S. NORTON, JR. PRESIDENT. Keyes opens the door. They go in.

10-4-43

INT. RECEPTION ROOM - MR. NORTON'S OFFICE

A secretary sitting behind a desk. As Keyes and Neff enter, the door to Norton's private office is opened. From inside, Mr. Norton is letting out three legal looking gentlemen. Norton is about forty-five, very well groomed, rather pompous in manner.

NORTON:
(To the men who are leaving)
I believe the legal position is now clear, gentlemen. Please stand by. I may need you later.

He sees Keyes and Neff.

NORTON:　Come in, Mr. Keyes. You too, Mr. Neff.

Neff has put down his hat and briefcase. He and Keyes pass the legal looking men and follow Norton into his office.

C-4　INT. NORTON'S OFFICE

Naturally it is the best office in the building; modern but not modernistic, spacious, very well furnished; flowers, smoking stands, easy chairs, etc. Norton has gone behind his desk. Keyes has come in, and Neff after him closes the door quietly. Norton looks disapprovingly at Keyes' shirt sleeves.

NORTON:　You find this an uncomfortably warm day Mr. Keyes?

Keyes takes his hat off but holds it in his hands.

KEYES:　Sorry, Mr. Norton. I didn't know this was formal.

Norton smiles frostily.

NORTON:
Sit down, gentlemen.
(To Keyes)
Any new developments?

Keyes and Neff sit down, Norton remains standing.

KEYES:　I just talked to this Jackson long distance. Up in Medford, Oregon.

NORTON:　Who's Jackson?

KEYES:
The last guy that saw Dietrichson alive. They were out on the observation platform together talking. Dietrichson wanted a cigar and Jackson went to get Dietrichson's cigar case for him. When he came back to the observation platform, no Dietrichson. Jackson didn't think anything was wrong until a wire caught up with the train at Santa Barbara. They had found Dietrichson's body on the tracks near Burbank.
(Continued)

C-4   (Cont'd)

NORTON: Very interesting, about the cigar case.

He walks up and down behind his desk thinking hard.

NORTON: Anything else?

KEYES: Not much. Dietrichson's secretary
says she didn't know anything about
the policy. There is a daughter, but
all she remembers is Neff talking to
her father about accident insurance at
their house one night.

NEFF: I couldn't sell him at first. Mrs.
Dietrichson opposed it. He told me he'd
think it over. Later on I went down to
the oil fields and closed him. He signed
the application and gave me his check.

NORTON: (Dripping with sarcasm)
A fine piece of salesmanship that was,
Mr. Neff.

KEYES: There's no sense in pushing Neff around.
He's got the best sales record in the
office. Are your salesmen supposed to
know that the customer is going to fall
off a train?

NORTON: Fall off a train? Are we sure Dietrichson
fell off the train?

There is a charged pause.

KEYES: I don't get it.

NORTON: You don't, Mr. Keyes? Then what do you
think of this case? This policy might
cost us a great deal of money. As you
know, it contains a double indemnity clause.
Just what is your opinion?

KEYES: No opinion at all.

NORTON: Not even a hunch? One of those interesting little hunches of yours?

KEYES: Nope. Not even a hunch.

NORTON: I'm surprised, Mr. Keyes. I've formed
a very definite opinion. I think I
know -- in fact I know I know what
happened to Dietrichson.

10-4-43   (Continued)

C-4   (Cont'd)

KEYES: You know you know what?

NORTON: I know it was not an accident.

He looks from Keyes to Neff and back to Keyes.

NORTON: What do you say to that?

KEYES: Me? You've got the ball. Let's
                      see you run with it.

NORTON: There's a widespread feeling that just
                      because a man has a large office --

The dictograph on his desk buzzes. He reaches over and de-
presses a key and puts the earpiece to his ear.

NORTON: (Into dictograph)
                      Yes?...Have her come in, please.

He replaces the earpiece. He turns back to Keyes and Neff.

NORTON: -- that just because a man has a
                      large office he must be an idiot.
                      I'm having a visitor, if you don't
                      mind.

Keyes and Neff start to get up.

NORTON: No, no. I want you to stay and
                      watch me handle this.

The secretary has opened the door.

SECRETARY: Mrs. Dietrichson.

Neff stands staring at the door. He relaxes with an obvious
effort of will. Phyllis comes in. She wears a gray tailored
suit, small black hat with a veil, black gloves, and carries
a black bag. The secretary closes the door behind her. Mr.
Norton goes to meet her.

NORTON: Thank you very much for coming, Mrs.
                      Dietrichson. I assure you I appreci-
                      ate it.

He turns a little towards Keyes.

NORTON: This is Mr. Keyes.

KEYES: How do you do.

PHYLLIS: How do you do.

C-4 (Cont'd)

NORTON: And Mr. Neff.

PHYLLIS: I've met Mr. Neff. How do you do.

Norton has placed a chair. Phyllis sits. Norton goes behind
his desk.

NORTON: Mrs. Dietrichson, I assure you of
                   our sympathy in your bereavement.
                   I hesitated before asking you to
                   come here so soon after your loss.

Phyllis nods silently.

NORTON: But now that you're here I hope you
                   won't mind if I plunge straight into
                   business. You know why we asked you
                   to come, don't you?

PHYLLIS: No. All I know is that your secretary
                   made it sound very urgent.

Keyes sits quietly in his chair with his legs crossed. He
has hung his hat on his foot and thrust his thumbs in the
armholes of his vest. He looks a little bored. Neff, behind him, stands leaning against the false mantel, completely
dead-pan.

NORTON: Your husband had an accident policy
                   with this company. Evidently you
                   don't know that, Mrs. Dietrichson.

PHYLLIS: No. I remember some talk at the
                   house --

She looks towards Neff.

PHYLLIS: -- but he didn't seem to want it.

NEFF: He took it out a few days later,
                   Mrs. Dietrichson.

PHYLLIS: I see.

NORTON: You'll probably find the policy
                   among his personal effects.

PHYLLIS: His safe deposit box hasn't been
                   opened yet. It seems a tax examiner
                   has to be present.

10-4-43   (Continued)

C-4 (Cont'd)

NORTON: Please, Mrs. Dietrichson, I don't
want you to think you are being
subjected to any questioning. But
there are a few things we should
like to know.

PHYLLIS: What sort of things?

NORTON: We have the report of the coroner's
inquest. Accidental death. We are
not entirely satisfied. In fact we
are not satisfied at all.

Phyllis looks at him coolly.
Keyes looks vaguely interested.
Neff is staring straight at Phyllis.

NORTON: Frankly, Mrs. Dietrichson, we suspect
suicide.

Phyllis doesn't bat an eyelash.

NORTON: I'm sorry. Would you like a glass
of water?

PHYLLIS: Please.

NORTON: Mr. Neff.

He indicates a thermos on a stand near Neff. Neff pours a
glass of water and carries it over to Phyllis. She has
lifted her veil a little. She takes the glass from his hand.

PHYLLIS: Thank you.

Their eyes meet for a fraction of a second.

NORTON: Had your husband been moody or depressed
lately, Mrs. Dietrichson? Did he seem
to have financial worries, for instance?

PHYLLIS: He was perfectly all right and I don't
know of any financial worries.

NORTON: There must have been something, Mrs.
Dietrichson. Let us examine this so-
called accident. First, your husband
takes out this policy in absolute
secrecy. Why? Because he doesn't
want his family to suspect what he
intends to do.

PHYLLIS: Do what?

10-4-43

(Continued)

C-4   (Cont'd)

NORTON: Commit suicide. Next, he goes on
this trip entirely alone. He has
to be alone. He hobbles all the
way out to the observation platform,
very unlikely with his leg in a
cast, unless he has a very strong
reason. Once there, he finds he
is not alone. There is a man there.
What was his name, Keyes?

Norton flips his fingers impatiently at Keyes who doesn't
even bother to look up.

KEYES: His name was Jackson. Probably still is.

NORTON: Jackson. So your husband gets rid of
this Jackson with some flimsy excuse
about cigars. And then he is alone.
And then he does it. He jumps. Suicide.
In which case the company is not liable.
         (Pause)
You know that, of course. We could
go to court --

PHYLLIS: I don't know anything. In fact I
don't know why I came here.

She makes as if to rise indignantly.

NORTON: Just a moment, please. I said we <u>could</u>
go to court. I didn't say we want to.
Not only is it against our practice, but
it would involve a great deal of expense,
a lot of lawyers, a lot of time, perhaps
years.

Phyllis rises coldly.

NORTON: So what I want to suggest is a compromise
on both sides. A settlement for a certain
sum, a part of the policy value --

PHYLLIS: Don't bother, Mr. Norton. When I came
in here I had no idea you owed me any
money. You told me you did. Then you
told me you didn't. Now you tell me you
want to pay me a part of it, whatever it
is. You want to bargain with me, at a
time like this. I don't like your in-
sinuations about my husband, Mr. Norton,
and I don't like your methods. In fact
I don't like you, Mr. Norton. Goodbye,gentlemen

She turns and walks out. The door closes after her. There is
a pregnant pause. Keyes straightens up in his chair.

10-4-43   (Continued)

C-4 (Cont'd)

KEYES: Nice going, Mr. Norton. You sure
       carried that ball.

Norton pours himself a glass of water and stands holding it.

KEYES: Only you fumbled on the goal line. Then
       you heaved an illegal forward pass and
       got thrown for a forty-yard loss. Now
       you can't pick yourself up because you
       haven't got a leg to stand on.

NORTON: I haven't eh? Let her claim. Let her
       sue. We can prove it was suicide.

Keyes stands up.

KEYES: Can we? Mr. Norton, the first thing
       that hit me was that suicide angle.
       Only I dropped it in the wastepaper
       basket just three seconds later. You
       ought to take a look at the statistics
       on suicide sometime. You might learn
       a little something about the insurance
       business.

NORTON: I was raised in the insurance business,
       Mr. Keyes.

KEYES: Yeah. In the front office. Come on,
       you never read an actuarial table in your
       life. I've got ten volumes on suicide
       alone. Suicide by race, by color, by
       occupation, by sex, by seasons of the
       year, by time of day. Suicide, how com-
       mitted: by poisons, by fire-arms, by
       drowning, by leaps. Suicide by poison,
       subdivided by types of poison, such as
       corrosive, irritant, systemic, gaseous,
       narcotic, alkaloid, protein, and so forth.
       Suicide by leaps, subdivided by leaps from
       high places, under wheels of trains, under
       wheels of trucks, under the feet of horses,
       from steamboats. But Mr. Norton, of all
       the cases on record there's not one single
       case of suicide by leap from the rear end
       of a moving train. And do you know how fast
       that train was going at the point where the
       body was found? Fifteen miles an hour.
       Now how could anybody jump off a slow mov-
       ing train like that with any kind of expec-
       tation that he would kill himself? No soap,
       Mr. Norton. We're sunk, and we're going to
       pay through the nose, and you know it. May
       I have this?

(Continued)

C-4 (Cont'd)

Keyes' throat is dry after the long speech. He grabs the
glass of water out of Norton's hand and drains it in one big
gulp.

Norton is watching him almost stupefied. Neff stands with
the shadow of a smile on his face. Keyes puts the glass
down noisily on Norton's desk.

KEYES: Come on, Walter.

Norton doesn't move or speak. Keyes puts his hat on and
crosses towards the door, Neff after him. With the doorknob in his hand Keyes turns back to Norton with a glance
down at his own shirt sleeves.

KEYES: Next time I'll rent a tuxedo.

They go out.

DISSOLVE TO:

C-5   NEFF - AT DICTAPHONE - (NIGHT)

There is a tired grin on his face as he talks into the horn.

NEFF: I could have hugged you right then and
                there, Keyes, you and your statistics.
                You were the only one we were really
                scared of, and instead you were almost
                playing on our team...

DISSOLVE TO:

C-6   NEFF'S APARTMENT - EVENING -
      ALMOST DARK IN THE ROOM   NEFF'S VOICE:
                                        That evening when I got home
The corridor door opens let-
ting light in. Neff enters   my nerves had eased off. I
with his hat on and his
briefcase under his arm. He   could feel the ground under
switches the lights on,
closes the door, puts the   my feet again, and it looked
lights on, closes the door,
puts the key in his pocket.   like easy going from there
At this moment the telephone
rings. He picks up the phone.   on in.

NEFF: Hello... Hello, baby....
                Sure, everything is fine...
                You were wonderful in Norton's office.

C-7   INT. TELEPHONE BOOTH IN A DRUG STORE

Phyllis is on the phone. She is not dressed as in Norton's
office.
10-4-43   (Continued)

C-7 (Cont'd)

> PHYLLIS: I felt so funny. I wanted to look at
>   you all the time.

C-8   NEFF ON TELEPHONE IN HIS APARTMENT

> NEFF: How do you think I felt?
>   Where are you, baby?

C-9   PHYLLIS ON PHONE

> PHYLLIS: At the drug store. Just a block away.
>   Can I come up?

C-10   NEFF'S APARTMENT - (NIGHT) - NEFF ON PHONE

> NEFF: Okay. But be careful. Don't
>   let anybody see you.

He hangs up, takes off his hat and drops hat and briefcase
on the davenport. He looks around the room and crosses to
lower the venetian blinds and draw the curtains. He gathers
up the morning paper which is lying untidily on the floor
and puts it in the waste-paper basket.

The door bell rings.

Neff stops in sudden alarm. It can't be Phyllis. The time
is too short. For a second he stands there motionless, then
crosses to the door and opens it.

In the open door stands Keyes.

> NEFF: Hello, Keyes.

Keyes walks past him into the room. His hands are clasped
behind his back. There is a strange, absent-minded look in
his eyes. Neff closes the door without taking his eyes off
Keyes.

> NEFF: What's on your mind?

Keyes stops in the middle of the room and turns.

> KEYES: That broken leg. The guy broke his leg.

> NEFF: What are you talking about?

> KEYES: Talking about Dietrichson. He had acci-
>   dent insurance, didn't he? Then he
>   broke his leg, didn't he?

> NEFF: So what?

10-4-43   (Continued)

C-10 (Cont'd)

KEYES: And he didn't put in a claim.
                Why didn't he put in a claim?
                Why?

NEFF: What the dickens are you driving
                at?

KEYES: Walter. There's something wrong.
                I ate dinner two hours ago. It
                stuck half way.

He prods his stomach with his thumb.

KEYES: The little man is acting up
                again. Because there's something
                wrong with that Dietrichson case.

NEFF: Because he didn't put in a claim?
                Maybe he just didn't have time.

KEYES: Oh maybe he just didn't know he
                was insured.

He has stopped in front of Neff. They look at each other
for a tense moment. Neff hardly breathes.

Keyes shakes his head suddenly.

KEYES: No. That couldn't be it.
                You delivered the policy to him
                personally, didn't you, Walter?
                And you got his check.

NEFF: (Stiff-lipped, but his
                              voice is as well under
                              control as he can manage)
                Sure, I did.

Keyes prods his stomach again.

KEYES: Got any bicarbonate of soda?

NEFF: No I haven't.

Keyes resumes his pacing.

KEYES: Listen, Walter. I've been living
                with this little man for twenty-six
                years. He's never failed me yet.
                There's got to be something wrong.

NEFF: Maybe Norton was right. Maybe it
                was suicide, Keyes.

10-4-43   (Continued)

85

C-10 (Cont'd)

KEYES: No. Not suicide.
                 (Pause)
            But not accident either.

NEFF: What else?

There is another longer pause, agonizing for Neff. Finally
Keyes continues:

KEYES: Look. A man takes out an accident
            policy that is worth a hundred thousand
            dollars if he is killed on a train.
            Then, two weeks later, he <u>is</u> killed on
            a train. And not in a tra<u>in</u> accident,
            mind you, but falling off some silly
            observation car. Do you know what the
            mathematical probability of that is,
            Walter? One out of I don't know how
            many billions. And add to that the
            broken leg. It just can't be the way
            it looks, Walter. Something has been
            worked on us.

NEFF: Such as what?

Keyes doesn't answer. He goes on pacing up and down.
Finally Neff can't stand the silence any longer.

NEFF: Murder?

KEYES: (Prods stomach again)
            Don't you have any peppermint or
            anything?

NEFF: I'm sorry.
                 (Pause)
            Who do you suspect?

KEYES: Maybe I like to make things easy
            for myself. But I always tend to
            suspect the beneficiary.

NEFF: The wife?

KEYES: Yeah. That wide-eyed dame that
            didn't know anything about anything.

NEFF: You're crazy, Keyes. She wasn't
            even on the train.

KEYES: I know she wasn't, Walter. I
            don't claim to know how it was
            worked, or who worked it, but I
            know that it <u>was</u> worked.

C-10 (Cont'd)

He crosses to the corridor door.

KEYES: I've got to get to a drug store.
It feels like a hunk of concrete
inside me.

He puts his hand on the knob to open the door.

C-11 CORRIDOR - APARTMENT HOUSE - NIGHT - LIGHTS ON

The hallway is empty except for Phyllis who has been standing
close to the door of Huff's apartment, listening. The door
has just started to open. Phyllis moves away quickly and
flattens herself against the wall behind the opening door.
Keyes is coming out.

KEYES: Good night, Walter.

Neff, behind him, looks anxiously down the hallway for
Phyllis. Suddenly his eye catches a glimpse of her through
the crack of the partly opened door. He pushes the door wide
so as to hide her from Keyes.

NEFF: Good night, Keyes.

KEYES: See you at the office in the morning.

He has reached the elevator. He pushes the call button and
turns.

KEYES: But I'd like to move in on her right
now, tonight, if it wasn't for Norton
and his stripe-pants ideas about company policy. I'd have the cops after
her so quick her head would spin.
They'd put her through the wringer,
and, brother, what they would squeeze
out.

NEFF: Only you haven't got a single thing
to go on, Keyes.

The elevator has come up and stopped.

KEYES: Not too much. Twenty-six years experience, all the percentage there
is, and this lump of concrete in my
stomach.

He pulls back the elevator door and turns to Neff with one
last glance of annoyance.

KEYES: (Almost angrily)
           No bicarbonate of soda.

10-4-43

                                 (Continued)

C-11 (Cont'd)

Keyes gets into the elevator. The door closes. The elevator goes down.

Neff stands numb, looking at the spot where Keyes was last visible. Without moving his eyes he pulls the door around towards him with his left hand. Phyllis slowly comes out.

Neff motions quickly to her to go into the apartment. She crosses in front of nim and enters. He steps in backwards after her.

C-12 INT. NEFF'S APARTMENT

Phyllis has come a few steps into the room. Neff, backing in after her, closes the door from inside and turns slowly. They look at each other for a long moment in complete silence.

PHYLLIS: How much does he know?

NEFF: It's not what he knows. It's those stinking hunches of his.

PHYLLIS: But he can't prove anything, can he?

NEFF: Not if we're careful. Not if we don't see each other for a while.

PHYLLIS: For how long a while?

She moves toward him but he does not respond.

NEFF: Until all this dies down. You don't know Keyes the way I do. Once he gets his teeth into something he won't let go. He'll investigate you. He'll have you shadowed. He'll watch you every minute from now on. Are you afraid, baby?

PHYLLIS: Yes, I'm afraid. But not of Keyes. I'm afraid of us. We're not the same any more. We did it so we could be together, but instead of that it's pulling us apart. Isn't it, Walter?

NEFF: What are you talking about?

PHYLLIS: And you don't really care whether we see each other or not.

NEFF: Shut up, baby.

He pulls her close and kisses her.

FADE OUT

END OF SEQUENCE "C"

FADE IN:

D-1   <u>INSURANCE OFFICE</u> - <u>TWELFTH FLOOR</u> - <u>ANTEROOM</u> - (DAY)

Two telephone operators and a receptionist are at work.
Several visitors are waiting in chairs. Lola Dietrichson
is one of them. She's wearing a simple black suit and hat,
indicating mourning. Her fingers nervously pick at a handkerchief and her eyes are watching the elevator doors
anxiously.

(Now and then the telephone operators in the background
are heard saying, "PACIFIC ALL-RISK. GOOD AFTERNOON.")

The elevator comes up and the doors open. Several people
come out, among them Neff, carrying his briefcase. Lola
sees him and stands up, and as he is about to pass through
the anteroom without recognizing her she stops him.

LOLA: Hello, Mr. Neff

Neff looks at her a little startled.

NEFF: Hello.

His voice hangs in the air.

LOLA: Lola Dietrichson. Don't you
                 remember me?

NEFF: (On his guard)
                 Yes. Of course.

LOLA: Could I talk to you, just for
                 a few minutes? Somewhere where
                 we can be alone?

NEFF: Sure. Come on into my office.

He pushes the swing door open and holds it for her. As she
passes in front of him his eyes narrow in uneasy specu-
lation.

D-2   <u>TWELFTH FLOOR</u> - <u>BALCONY</u>

Neff comes up level with Lola and leads her towards his
office, CAMERA WITH THEM.

NEFF: Is it something to do with --
                 what happened?

LOLA: Yes, Mr. Neff. It's about my
                 father's death.

D-2 (Cont'd)

NEFF: I'm terribly sorry, Miss Dietrichson.

He opens the door of his office and holds it for her.
She enters.

D-3   INT. NEFF'S OFFICE - (DAY)

Lou Schwartz, one of the other salesmen, is working at his
desk. Lola enters, Neff after her.

NEFF: (To Schwartz)
               Lou, do you mind if I use the
               office alone for a few minutes?

SCHWARTZ: It's all yours, Walter.

He gets up and goes out. Lola has walked over to the window
and is looking out so Schwartz won't stare at her. Neff
places a chair beside his desk.

NEFF: Won't you sit down?

At the sound of the closing door she turns and speaks with
a catch in her voice.

LOLA: Mr. Neff, I can't help it,
               but I have such a strange
               feeling that there is something
               queer about my father's death.

NEFF: Queer? Queer in what way?

LOLA: I don't know why I should be
               bothering you with my troubles,
               except that you knew my father
               and knew about the insurance
               he took out. And you were so
               nice to me that evening in your
               car.

NEFF: Sure. We got along fine, didn't
               we.

He sits down. His face is grim and watchful.

LOLA: Look at me, Mr. Neff. I'm not
               crazy. I'm not hysterical. I'm
               not even crying. But I have the
               awful feeling that something is
               wrong, and I had the same feeling
               once before - when my mother died.

10-12-43

                                              (Continued)

D-3   (Cont'd)

NEFF: When your mother died?

LOLA: We were up at Lake Arrowhead.
That was six years ago. We had
a cabin there. It was winter and
very cold and my mother was very
sick with pneumonia. She had a
nurse with her. There were just the
three of us in the cabin. One night
I got up and went into my mother's room.
She was delirious with fever. All the
bed covers were on the floor and the
windows were wide open. The nurse
wasn't in the room. I ran and covered
my mother up as quickly as I could.
Just then I heard a door open behind
me. The nurse stood there. She didn't
say a word, but there was a look in her
eyes I'll never forget. Two days later
my mother was dead.
          (Pause)
Do you know who that nurse was?

Neff stares at her tensely. He knows only too well who the
nurse was.

NEFF: No. Who?

LOLA: Phyllis. I tried to tell my father,
but I was just a kid then and he
wouldn't listen to me. Six months
later she married him and I kind of
talked myself out of the idea that she
could have done anything like that.
But now it's all back again, now that
something has happened to my father, too.

NEFF: You're not making sense, Miss Dietrichson.
Your father fell off a train.

LOLA: Yes, and two days before he fell
off that train what was Phyllis doing?
She was in her room in front of a
mirror, with a black hat on, and she
was pinning a black veil to it, as
if she couldn't wait to see how she
would look in mourning.

NEFF: Look. You've had a pretty bad
shock. Aren't you just imagining
all this?

10-12-43   (Continued)

LOLA: I caught her eyes in the mirror,
               and they had that look in them
               they had before my mother died.
               That same look.

NEFF: You don't like your step-mother,
               do you? Isn't it just because
               she is your step-mother?

LOLA: I loathe her. Because she did it.
               She did it for the money. Only
               you're not going to pay her, are
               you, Mr. Neff? She's not going
               to get away with it this time.
               I'm going to speak up. I'm going
               to tell everything I know.

NEFF: You'd better be careful, saying
               things like that.

LOLA: I'm not afraid. You'll see.

She turns again to the window so he won't see that she is
crying. Neff gets up and goes to her.

LOLA: I'm sorry. I didn't mean to
               act like this.

NEFF: All this that you've been telling
               me --- who else have you told?

LOLA: No one.

NEFF: How about your step-mother?

LOLA: Of course not. I'm not living in
               the house any more. I moved out.

NEFF: And you didn't tell that boy-
               friend of yours? Zacchetti.

LOLA: I'm not seeing him any more. We
               had a fight.

NEFF: Where are you living then?

LOLA: I got myself a little apartment
               in Hollywood.

NEFF: Four walls, and you just sit and
               look at them, huh?

D-3   (Cont'd)

She turns from the window with a pathetic little nod.

LOLA: (Through her tears)
         Yes, Mr. Neff.

DISSOLVE TO:

D-4   LA GOLONDRINA (NIGHT)   NEFF'S VOICE

In the foreground, Neff and Lola are having dinner. In the background the usual activity of Olvera Street -- sidewalk peddlers, guitar players, etc.	So I took her to dinner that evening at a Mexican joint down on Olvera Street where nobody would see us.

DISSOLVE TO:

I wanted to cheer her up..

D-5   INT. NEFF'S COUPE (DAY)

Next day was Sunday and we

Neff and Lola driving along the beach near Santa Monica. Neff is wearing a light summer suit, very much in contrast to Lola's mourning. Apparently she is telling him a story and now and then she laughs, but there is no sound. CAMERA MOVES PAST HER TO A:	went for a ride down to the beach. She had loosened up a bit and she was even laughing...I had to make sure she wouldn't tell that
CLOSE SHOT OF NEFF behind the stearing wheel. He is only half listening to Lola. His mind is full of other thoughts.	stuff about Phyllis to anybody else. It was dynamite, whether it was true or not.

And I had no chance to talk

to Phyllis. You were watch-

ing her like a hawk, Keyes.

I couldn't even phone her

for fear you had the wires

tapped.

D-6   INSURANCE OFFICE -
12TH FLOOR - DAY

Neff, with his hat on and no briefcase, is walking toward Keyes' office. As he comes up close to the door, he stops with a startled expression on his face. On a chair beside the door sits a familiar figure. He is Jackson, the man from the observation platform of the train. He is wearing his Stetson hat and smoking a cigar. He is studying something in the file folder. Neff recognizes him immediately but Jackson does not look up. Neff controls his expression and goes on to open the door to Keyes' office.	NEFF'S VOICE Monday morning there was a note on my desk that you wanted to see me, Keyes. For a minute I wondered if it could be about Lola. It was worse. Outside your door was the last guy in the world I wanted to see.

D-7   INT. KEYES' OFFICE

Neff is just closing the door from the inside. Keyes, his coat off, is lying on his office couch, chewing on a cigar, as usual.

KEYES: Come in. Come in, Walter. I want to ask you something. After all the years we've known each other, do you mind if I make a rather blunt statement?

NEFF: About what?

KEYES: About me. Walter, I'm a very great man. This Dietrichson business. It's murder, and murders don't come any neater. As fancy a piece of homicide as anybody ever ran into. Smart and tricky and almost perfect, but - -

Keyes bounces off the couch like a rubber ball.

KEYES: - - but, I think Papa has it all figured out, figured out and wrapped up in tissue paper with pink ribbons on it.

NEFF: I'm listening.

Keyes levels a finger at him.

KEYES: You know what? That guy Dietrichson was never on the train.

NEFF: He wasn't?

(Continued)

KEYES: No, he wasn't, Walter. Look, you
can't be sure of killing a man by
throwing him off a train that's
going fifteen miles an hour. The
only way you can be sure is to kill
him first and then throw his body on
the tracks. That would mean either
killing him on the train, or -- and
this is where it really gets fancy --
you kill him somewhere else and put him
on the tracks. Two possibilities, and
I personally buy the second.

NEFF: You're way ahead of me, Keyes.

KEYES: Look, it was like this. They killed
the guy -- the wife and somebody else --
and then the somebody else took the
crutches and went on the train as
Dietrichson, and then the somebody else
jumped off, and then they put the body
on the tracks where the train had passed.
An impersonation, see. And a cinch to
work. Because it was night, very few
people were about, they had the crutches
to stare at, and they never really looked
at the man at all.

NEFF: It's fancy all right, Keyes. Maybe it's
a little too fancy.

KEYES: Is it? I tell you it fits together like
a watch. And now let's see what we have
in the way of proof. The only guy that
really got a good look at this supposed
Dietrichson is sitting right outside my
office. I took the trouble to bring him
down here from Oregon. Let's see what he
has to say.

Keyes goes to the door and opens it.

KEYES: Come in, Mr. Jackson.

Jackson enters with the file folder.

JACKSON: Yes sir, Mr. Keyes. These are fine
cigars you smoke.

He indicates the cigar he himself is smoking.

KEYES: Two for a quarter.

JACKSON: That's what I said.

                               (Continued)

D-7   (Cont'd)

KEYES: Never mind the cigar, Jackson.
                          Did you study those photographs?
                          What do you say?

JACKSON: Yes, indeed, I studied them
                          thoroughly. Very thoroughly

KEYES: Well? Did you make up your mind?

JACKSON: Mr. Keyes, I'm a Medford man.
                          Medford, Oregon. Up in Medford we
                          take our time making up our minds --

KEYES: Well you're not in Medford now;
                          I'm in a hurry. Let's have it.

Jackson indicates the file folder he is holding.

JACKSON: Are these photographs of the **l**ate
                          Mr. Dietrichson?

KEYES: Yes.

JACKSON: Then my answer is no.

KEYES: What do you mean no?

JACKSON: I mean this is not the man that
                          was on the train.

KEYES: Will you swear to that?

JACKSON: I'm a Medford man. Medford, Oregon.
                          And if I say it, I mean it, and if I
                          mean it, of course I'll swear it.

KEYES: Thank you.

Keyes turns to Neff.

KEYES: There you are, Walter. There's
                          your proof.

Keyes remembers he forgot to introduce Jackson.

KEYES: Oh, Mr. Jackson, this is Mr. Neff,
                          one of our salesmen.

JACKSON: Please to meet you, Mr. Neff.
                          Pleased indeed.

NEFF: How do you do.

D-7 (Cont'd)

JACKSON: Very fine, thank you. Never was
       better.

KEYES: Mr. Jackson, how would you describe
       the man you saw on that observation
       platform?

JACKSON: Well, I'm pretty sure he was a younger
       man, about ten or fifteen years younger
       than the man in these photographs.

KEYES: Dietrichson was about fifty, wasn't he,
       Walter?

NEFF: Fifty-one, according to the policy.

JACKSON: The man I saw was nothing like fifty-
       one years old. Of course, it was pretty
       dark on that platform and, come to think
       of it, he tried to keep his back towards
       me. But I'm positive just the same.

KEYES: That's fine, Jackson. Now you understand
       this matter is strictly confidential. We
       may need you again down here in Los
       Angeles, if the case comes to court.

JACKSON: Any time you need me, I'm at your entire
       disposal, gentlemen. Expenses paid, of
       course.

Keyes picks up the telephone on his desk and speaks into it.

KEYES: Get me Lubin, in the cashier's office.

Meanwhile, Jackson crosses over to Neff and, during the ensuing dialogue between him and Neff, we hear Keyes' low voice
on the phone in background. We do not hear what he says.

JACKSON: (To Neff)
       Ever been in Medford, Mr. Neff?

NEFF: Never.

JACKSON: Wait a minute. Do you go trout
       fishing? Maybe I saw you up
       Klamath Falls way.

NEFF: Nope. Never fish.

JACKSON: Neff. Neff. I've got it! It's
       the name. There's a family of Neffs
       in Corvallis.

10-12-43   (Continued)

AB   11-27-43   <u>DOUBLE INDEMNITY</u>   D-10
                                                              (92)
D-7   (Cont'd)

NEFF: No relation.

JACKSON: Let me see. This man's an automobile
dealer in Corvallis. Very reputable
man, too, I'm told.

Keyes rejoins them at this point.

KEYES: All right, Mr. Jackson. Suppose you
go down to the cashier's office --
room twenty-seven on the eleventh floor.
They'll take care of your expense account
and your ticket for the train tonight.

JACKSON: Tonight? Tomorrow morning would suit
me better. There's a very good osteo-
path down here I want to see before I
leave.

Keyes has opened the door for Jackson.

KEYES: Okay, Mr. Jackson. Just don't put
her on the expense account.

Jackson doesn't get it.

JACKSON: Goodbye, gentlemen. A pleasure.

He goes out.

KEYES: There it is, Walter. It's beginning
to come apart at the seams already. A
murder's never perfect. It always comes
apart sooner or later. And when two
people are involved it's usually sooner.
We know the Dietrichson dame is in it,
and somebody else. Pretty soon we're
going to know who that somebody else is.
He'll show. He's got to show. Sometime,
somewhere, they've got to meet. Their
emotions are all kicked up. Whether it's
love or hate doesn't matter. They can't
keep away from each other. They think it's
twice as safe because there are two of them.
But it's not twice as safe. It's ten times
twice as dangerous. They've committed a
murder and that's not like taking a trolley
ride together where each one can get off at
a different stop. They're stuck with each
other. They've got to ride all the way to
the end of the line. And it's a one-way
trip, and the last stop is the cemetery.

                                                       (Continued)

D-7 (Cont'd)

He puts a cigar in his mouth and starts tapping his pockets
for matches.

KEYES: (Continued)
                  She put in her claim and I'm going to
                  throw it right back at her.
                    (Pats his pockets again)
                  Have you got one of those?

Neff strikes a match for him. Keyes takes the match out
of his hand and lights his cigar.

KEYES: Let her sue us if she dares. I'll be
                  ready for her -- and that somebody else.
                  They'll be digging their own graves.

DISSOLVE TO:

D-8   <u>TELEPHONE BOOTH IN JERRY'S MARKET</u> - DAY

Neff is in the booth dialing a number, and as she waits he looks around to make sure he is not watched.

NEFF: (Into phone)
                  Mrs. Dietrichson?... This is Jerry's market. We just got in a shipment of that English soap you were asking about. Will you be coming by this morning?... Thank you, Mrs. Dietrichson.

Neff hangs up.

DISSOLVE TO:

D-9   <u>EXT. JERRY'S MARKET</u> - DAY

The LaSalle stops in front of the market. Phyllis steps out and goes into the market, looking around.

D-10   <u>SHELVES IN THE REAR OF MARKET</u>

Neff is moving slowly along the shelves, outwardly calm but with his nerves on edge. From beyond him Phyllis approaches. She stops beside him, facing the same way, with a couple of feet separating them.

PHYLLIS: Hello, Walter.

NEFF: (In a harsh whisper)
                  Come closer.

Phyllis moves close to him.

PHYLLIS: What's the matter?

NEFF: Everything's the matter. Keyes is rejecting your claim. He's sitting back with his mouth watering, waiting for you to sue. He wants you to sue. But you're not going to.

PHYLLIS: What's he got to stop me?

NEFF: He's got the goods. He's figured out how it was worked. He knows it was somebody else on the train. He's dug up a witness he thinks will prove it.

PHYLLIS: Prove it how? Listen, if he rejects that claim, I <u>have</u> to sue.

NEFF: Yeah? And then you're in court and a lot of other things are going to come up. Like, for instance, about you and the first Mrs. Dietrichson.

10-25-43   (Continued)

Phyllis looks at him sharply, sideways.

PHYLLIS: What about me and the first Mrs.
              Dietrichson?

NEFF: The way she died. And about that black
              hat you were trying on --- before you
              needed a black hat.

A customer comes along the aisle toward them. They move
apart. The customer passes. Phyllis draws close again.

PHYLLIS: Walter, Lola's been telling you some of
              her cockeyed stories. She's been seeing
      .   you.

NEFF: I've been seeing her, if you want to
              know. So she won't yell her head off
              about what she knows.

PHYLLIS: Yes, she's been putting on an act for
              you, crying all over your shoulder,
              that lying little ---

NEFF: Keep her out of it. All I'm telling
              you is we're not going to sue.

PHYLLIS: Because you don't want the money any
              more, even if you could get it? Because
              she's made you feel like a heel all of
              sudden.

NEFF: It isn't the money any more. It's our
              necks now. We're pulling out, understand.

PHYLLIS: Because of what Keyes can do? You're not
              fooling me, Walter. It's because of Lola.
              What you did to her father. You can't
              take it that she might find out some
              day.

NEFF: I said, leave her out of it.

PHYLLIS: Walter, it's me I'm talking about. I
              don't want to be left out of it.

NEFF: Stop saying that. It's just that it
              hasn't worked out the way we wanted. We
              can't have the money. We can't go through
              with it, that's all.

D-10 (Cont'd)

PHYLLIS: We have gone through with it, Walter.
                     The tough part is all behind us.
                     We just have to hold on now and not
                     go soft inside, and stick together,
                     close, the way we atarted out.

Phyllis takes his arm, forgetting where she is. He pulls
away.

NEFF: Watch it, will you. Someone's coming.

One of the market help, pushing a small hand-truck loaded
with packaged goods, comes along the aisle. He stops and
begins to restock a shelf very close to Neff and Phyllis.
They go off slowly in opposite directions. CAMERA PANS with
Neff as he walks toward another shelf, one that stands away
from the wall. Phyllis appears on the opposite side of the
shelf and stops, facing toward him. They now continue their
low-voiced dialogue through the piled-up merchandise.

PHYLLIS: I loved you, Walter. And I hated
                     him. But I wasn't going to do any-
                     thing about it, not until I met you.
                     It was you had the plan. I only
                     wanted him dead.

NEFF: Yeah, and I was the one that fixed
                     him so he was dead. Is that what
                     you're telling me?

Phyllis takes off her dark glasses for the first time and
looks at him with cold, hard eyes.

PHYLLIS: Yes. And nobody's pulling out. We
                     went into it together, and we're
                     coming out at the end together. It's
                     straight down the line for both of
                     us, remember.

Phyllis puts the glasses on again and goes.

Over Neff's face, as   NEFF'S VOICE
he looks after her,
comes the COMMENTARY.   Yeah. I remembered all right.
                     Just as I remembered what you
                     had told me, Keyes, about that
                     trolley car ride and how there
                     was no way to get off -- until
                     the end of the line.

DISSOLVE:

10-25-43

D-11   <u>INT. NEFF'S OFFICE</u> - (NIGHT)

Neff is dictating into the dictaphone.

NEFF: Yeah, I remembered it all right.
Just as I remembered what you had
told me, Keyes, about that trolley
car ride, and how there was no way
to get off until the end of the line,
where the cemetery was. And I got
to thinking what cemeteries are for.
They're to put dead people in, I
guess that was the first time I ever
thought about Phyllis that way. Dead,
I mean, and how things would be if she
was dead. Because the way it was now
she had me by the throat. She could
hang me higher than a kite any day
she felt like it. And there was
nothing I could do, except hold my
breath and watch that day come closer
and closer, and maybe pray a little,
if I still knew how to pray...
I saw Lola three or four times that
week. I guess it sounds crazy,
Keyes, after what I had done, but it
was only with her that I could relax
and let go a little. Then one night
we drove up into the hills above
Hollywood Bowl...

DISSOLVE TO:

D-12   <u>HOLLYWOOD HILLS</u> (NIGHT)(TRANSPARENCY)

Neff and Lola are climbing over a low hill in the foreground.
The sky is starlit and music from the Bowl comes over the
scene from below (Cesar Franck D Minor Symphony). As he
helps her climb up, CAMERA PANS with them and shows the
expanse of the Bowl below, a packed audience, and the
orchestra on the lighted shell.

They sit down on the grass. Neff sits near her, not too
close. It is very dark and they are silhouetted against
the shell lights. Neff puts a cigarette in his mouth and
strikes a match. The flame lights up Lola's face. Neff
glances at her. She is crying. He lights his cigarette
and blows out the match. A pause follows.

NEFF: Why are you crying?

Lola doesn't answer.

NEFF: You won't tell me?

11-27-43   (Continued)

D-12   (Cont'd)

LOLA: (In a choked voice)
                         Of course I will, Walter. I wouldn't
                         tell anybody else but you. It's
                         about Nino.

NEFF: Zachette? What about him?

LOLA: They killed my father together. He
                         and Phyllis. He helped her do it.
                         I know he did.

NEFF: What makes you say that?

LOLA: I've been following him. He's at
                         her house, night after night. It
                         was Phyllis and him all the time.
                         Maybe he was going with me just for
                         a blind. And the night of the murder --

NEFF: You promised not to talk that way
                         any more.

LOLA: -- he was supposed to pick me up
                         after a lecture at U.C.L.A. - but
                         he never showed up. He said he was
                         sick. Sick! He couldn't show up,
                         because the train was leaving with
                         my father on it.

She begins to cry again.

LOLA: Maybe I'm just crazy. Maybe it's
                         all just in my mind.

NEFF: Sure, it's all in your mind.

LOLA: I only wish it was, Walter, because
                         I still love him.

Over Neff's face, as he   NEFF'S VOICE
listens to the music,   Zachette. That's funny.
comes the commentary.   Phyllis and Zachette. What
                             was he doing up at her house?
DISSOLVE TO: I couldn't figure that one out.
                             I tried to make sense out of
D-13   LOBBY OF PACIFIC BLDG. (DAY)   it and got nowhere. But the
                             real brain-twister came the
About 5:00 P.M. or a little next day. You sprang it on
later. A stream of office   me, Keyes, after office hours,
employees is coming out of   when you caught me down in
an elevator; a second ele-   the lobby of the building.
vator reaches the lobby and
some more office employees
come out, among them Neff,
wearing his hat and carrying
his briefcase.   (Continued)

CAMERA PRECEDES HIM as he walks toward the entrance doors.
He is stopped by Keyes' voice, off to one side.

KEYES'
VOICE: Oh, Walter, just a minute.

Neff stops and looks towards the cigar counter, as he moves
towards him. Keyes is standing there buying cigars. He is
stuffing them into his pockets.

NEFF: Hello, Keyes.

KEYES: Hang onto your hat, Walter.

NEFF: What for?

KEYES: Nothing much. The Dietrichson case
                  just busted wide open.

NEFF: How do you mean?

KEYES: The guy showed. That's how.

NEFF: The sombody else?

KEYES: Yeah. The guy that did it with her.

NEFF: No kidding?

KEYES: She's filed suit against us, and
                  it's okay by me. When we get into
                  that courtroom I'll tear them apart,
                  both of them. Come on -- I'll buy
                  you a martini.

NEFF: No thanks, Keyes.

KEYES: With two olives.

NEFF: I've got to get a shave and a shoe-
                  shine. I've got a date.

KEYES: Margie, I still bet she drinks
                  from the bottle.

He bites off the end of the cigar and puts the cigar into
his mouth. He starts tapping his pockets for a match, as
usual. Neff strikes a match for him.

NEFF: They give you matches when they
                  sell you cigars, Keyes. All you
                  have to do is ask for them.

11-27-43   (Continued)

D-13 (Cont'd)

KEYES: I don't like them. They always ex-
                plode in my pockets. So long, Walter.

Keyes goes toward the street   NEFF'S VOICE
and OUT OF SCENE. Neff moves   You sure had me worried, Keyes.
back into the lobby, CAMERA   I didn't know if you were play-
FOLLOWING HIM. As he reaches   ing cat-and-mouse with me, whe-
the elevator, he looks back   ther you knew all along I was
over his shoulder, to make   the somebody else. That's what
sure Keyes is gone, then steps   I had to find out, and I though
into the empty elevator.   I knew where to look . . .

NEFF: (to elevator operator)
                Twelve.

DISSOLVE TO:

D-14   ENTRANCE - OFFICE, 12TH FLOOR
        RECEPTION ROOM (DAY)   NEFF'S VOICE
                                            Upstairs, the last of the
Neff comes out of the elevat-   people were just leaving.
or. The receptionist is just
tidying up her desk. She has
her hat on and is preparing
to leave. Neff passes on
through the swinging doors to
the twelfth floor balcony.

D-15   12TH FLOOR BALCONY

Neff enters from the reception   NEFF'S VOICE
room. A couple of belated em-   I made sure nobody saw me go
ployees are leaving for the   into your office.
day. Neff goes toward Keyes'
office, looks around to make
sure he is unobserved, enters.

D-16   KEYES' OFFICE (DAY)

Neff has just come in. He goes over to Keyes' desk and searches
the papers on it. He tries the desk drawers and finds them
locked. His eye falls on the dictaphone on the stand beside
the desk. A record is on it, the needle is about two-thirds
of the way towards the end. He lifts the needle and sets it
back to the beginning of the record, sets the switch to play-
back position. He lifts the arm off the bracket and starts the
machine. Keyes' voice is heard coming from the horn:

KEYES'   (From dictaphone)
VOICE: Memo to Mr. Norton. Confidential.
                Dietrichson File. With regard to your
                proposal to put Walter Neff under sur-
                veillance, I disagree absolutely. I have
                investigated his movements on the night of
                the crime, and he is definitely placed in
                his apartment from 7:15 P.M. on. In addition
                to this, I have known Neff intimately for
                eleven years, and I personally vouch for
                him, without reservation ...
                                            (Cont'd)

D-16   (Cont'd)

Neff stops the machine. He sits down slowly, still holding the horn. He is deeply moved. After a moment, he
presses the switch again.

KEYES'   (From dictaphone)
VOICE: ....Furthermore, no connection whatso-
                    ever has been established between
                    Walter Neff and Mrs. Phyllis Dietrichson,
                    whereas I am now able to report that such
                    a connection has been established between
                    her and another man. This man has been
                    observed to visit the Dietrichson home on
                    the night of July 9th, 10th, 11th, 12th
                    and 13th. We have succeeded in identifying
                    him as one Nino Zachette, former medical
                    student, aged twenty-eight, residing at
                    Lilac Court Apartments 1228½ N. La Brea
                    Avenue. We have checked Zachette's move-
                    ments on the night of the crime and have
                    found that they cannot be accounted for.
                    I am preparing a more detailed report for
                    your consideration and it is my belief
                    that we already have sufficient evidence
                    against Zachette and Mrs. Dietrichson to
                    justify police action. I strongly urge
                    that this whole matter be turned over to
                    the office of the District Attorney.
                    Respectfully, Barton Keyes.

Neff sits, staring blankly at the wall. The cylinder goes
on revolving, but no more voice comes - only the whir of
the needle on the empty record. At last he remembers to
replace the horn. He hangs it back on its hook. The
machine stops. Neff gets up from the chair, walks slowly
to the door and goes out.

D-17   <u>12TH FLOOR, BALCONY</u>

Neff has just come out of Keyes' office. He walks slowly
back towards the reception room entrance, then stands there
looking out through the glass doors. All the employees have
now left. Neff is entirely alone. He moves as if to go
out, then stops rigidly as his face lights up with excite-
ment of a sudden idea. He turns quickly and walks on to
his own office and enters.

D-18   <u>NEFF'S OFFICE</u> (DAY)

Neff walks across to his desk, lifts the telephone and
dials a number. (During the ensuing telephone conversation,
only what he says is heard. The pauses indicate speeches
at the other end of the line).

11-27-43   (Continued)

D-18   (Cont'd)

NEFF: Phyllis? Walter. I've got to see
                you...Tonight...Yes, it has to be
                tonight...How's eleven o'clock?
                Don't worry about Keyes. He's satis-
                fied...Leave the door on the latch
                and put the lights out. No, nobody's
                watching the house...I told you Keyes
                is satisfied. It's just for the
                neighbors...That's what I said. Yeah,
                Eleven o'clock. Goodbye, baby.

Neff hangs up and stands
beside the desk with a
grim expression on his
face, takes a handker-   NEFF'S VOICE
chief out and wipes per-   I guess I don't have to tell
spiration from his fore-   you what I was going to do
head and the palms of   at eleven o'clock, Keyes.
his hands. The gesture   For the first time I saw a
has a symbolic quality,   way to get clear of the whole
as if he were trying to   mess I was in, and of Phyllis,
wipe away the murder.   too, all at the same time.
Over his face comes the   Yeah, that's what I thought.
commentary.   But what I didn't know was
                              that she was all set for me.
DISSOLVE TO: That she had outsmarted me
                              again, just like she always
D-19   HALL STAIRWAY OF   had...
        DIETRICHSON HOME (NIGHT)

The lights are turned on.   She was all set and waiting
Phyllis is coming down
the stairs. She wears   for me. It could have been
white lounging pajamas,
and she is carrying some-   something in my voice when I
thing small and heavy
concealed in a scarf in   called her up that tipped her
her right hand. She
reaches the front door,   off. And it could have been
opens it slightly, fixes
the catch so that the door   that she had the idea already.
can be opened from outside.
She switches off the porch   And an idea wasn't the only
light and the hall light.
She moves towards the living thing she had waiting for me.
room, where there is still
light on.

11-27-43

D-20   LIVING ROOM

On the long table behind the davenport, one of the lamps is
lit. The only other light in the room is a standing lamp beside the desk. A window toward the back is open, and through
it comes the SOUNDS OF MUSIC, probably a neighboring radio.

Phyllis enters and crosses to the table. She puts out the
lamp, then moves over to the desk and puts out the lamp there.
The room is filled with bright moonlight coming in at the
windows.

Phyllis crosses to the chair by the fireplace (the one she
sat in the first time Neff came to the house). She lifts
the loose cushion and puts what was in the scarf behind it.
As she withdraws the scarf, there is a brief glint of something metallic before she covers the hidden object with
the cushion again.

She turns to the low table in front of the davenport and
takes a cigarette from the box. She takes a match and is
about to strike it when, just then, she hears a car coming
up the hill. She listens, motionless. The car stops. A
car door is slammed.

Calmly, Phyllis strikes the match and lights her cigarette.
She drops the match casually into a tray, goes back to the
chair, sits down and waits, quietly smoking. There are footsteps outside the house.

Over the chair in which Phyllis is sitting, the hallway is
visible through the arch. The front door opens. Neff comes
in. He is silhouetted against the moonlight as he stands
there. He closes the door again.

PHYLLIS: (In foreground)
                In here, Walter.

Neff comes through the arch and walks slowly towards her.

NEFF: Hello, baby. Anybody else in the
                house?

PHYLLIS: Nobody. Why?

NEFF: What's that music?

PHYLLIS: A radio up the street.

Neff sits down on the arm of the davenport, close to her.

NEFF: Just like the first time I was
                here. We were talking about auto-
                mobile insurance. Only you were
                thinking about murder. And I was
                thinking about that anklet.

D-20   (Cont'd)

PHYLLIS: And what are you thinking about
               now?

NEFF: I'm all through thinking. This
               is goodbye.

PHYLLIS: Goodbye? Where are you going?

NEFF: It's you that's going, baby. Not
               me. I'm getting off the trolley
               car right at this corner.

PHYLLIS: Suppose you stop being fancy. Let's
               have it, whatever it is.

NEFF: I have a friend who's got a funny
               theory. He says when two people
               commit a murder they're kind of on
               a trolley car, and one can't get off
               without the other. They're stuck
               with each other. They have to go
               on riding clear to the end of the
               line. And the last stop is the
               cemetery.

PHYLLIS: Maybe he's got something there.

NEFF: You bet he has. Two people are
               going to ride to the end of the
               line, all right. Only I'm not
               going to be one of them. I've got
               another guy to finish my ride for
               me.

PHYLLIS: So you've got it all arranged, Walter.

NEFF: You arranged it for me. I didn't
               have to do a thing.

PHYLLIS: Just who are you talking about?

NEFF: An acquaintance of yours. A Mr.
               Zachette. Come on, baby, I just
               got into this because I knew a
               little something about insurance,
               didn't I? I was just a sucker.
               I'd have been brushed-off as soon
               as you got your hands on the money.

PHYLLIS: What are you talking about?

NEFF: Save it. I'm telling this. It's
               been you and that Zachette guy
               all along, hasn't it?

11-27-43

                                          (Continued)

D-20   (Cont'd)

PHYLLIS: That's not true.

NEFF: It doesn't make any difference
whether it's true or not. The
point is Keyes believes Zachette
is the guy he's been looking for.
He'll have him in that gas chamber
before he knows what happened to him.

PHYLLIS: And what's happening to me all this
time?

NEFF: Don't be silly. What do you expect
to happen to you? You helped him
do the murder, didn't you? That's
what Keyes thinks. And what's good
enough for Keyes is good enough for me.

PHYLLIS: Maybe it's not good enough for me,
Walter. Maybe I don't go for the idea.
Maybe I'd rather talk.

NEFF: Sometimes people are where they
can't talk. Under six feet of dirt,
for instance. And if it was you,
they'd just charge it up to Zachette,
wouldn't they. One more item on his
account. Sure they would. That's
just what they're going to do. Es-
pecially since he's coming here.
tonight...Oh, in about fifteen minutes
from now, baby. With the cops right
behind him. It's all taken care of.

PHYLLIS: And that'd make everything lovely
for you, wouldn't it?

NEFF: Right. And it's got to be done
before that suit of yours comes to
trial, and Lola gets a chance to
sound off, and they trip you up on
the stand, and you start to fold
up and drag me down with you.

PHYLLIS: Listen, Walter. Maybe I had Zachette
here so they won't get a chance to
trip me up. So we can get that
money and be together.

NEFF: That's cute. Say it again.

PHYLLIS: He came here the first time just
             to ask where Lola was. I made him
             come back. I was working on him.
             He's crazy sort of guy, quick-
             tempered. I kept hammering into him
             that she was with another man, so
             he'd get into one of his jealous
             rages, and then I'd tell him where
             she was. And you know what he'd
             have done to her, don't you, Walter.

NEFF: Yeah, and for once I believe you.
             Because it's just rotten enough.

PHYLLIS: We're both rotten, Walter.

NEFF: Only you're just a little more rotten.
             You're rotten clear through. You got
             me to take care of your husband, and
             then you got Zachette to take care of
             Lola, and maybe take care of me too,
             and then somebody else would have come
             along to take care of Zachette for you.
             That's the way you operate isn't it, baby.

PHYLLIS: Suppose it is, Walter. Is what you've
             cooked up for tonight any better?

Neff gets up from the davenport. He listens to the music
for a moment.

NEFF: I don't like this music anymore.
             It's too close. Do you mind if
             I shut the window?

Phyllis just stares at him. He goes quietly over to the
window and shuts it and draws the curtain. Phyllis speaks
to his back:

PHYLLIS: (Her voice low and urgent)
             Walter!

Neff turns, something changes in his face. There is the report of a gun. He stands motionless for a moment, then very
slowly starts towards her. CAMERA IS SHOOTING OVER HIS
SHOULDER at Phyllis as she stands with the gun in her hand.
Neff stops after he has taken a few steps.

NEFF: What's the matter? Why don't you
             shoot again? Maybe if I came a
             little closer?

D-20 (Cont'd)

Neff takes a few more steps towards her and stops again.

NEFF: How's that. Do you think you
                     can do it now?

Phyllis is silent. She doesn't shoot. Her expression is tortured. Neff goes on until he is close to her. Quietly he takes the gun out of her unresisting hand.

NEFF: Why didn't you shoot, baby?

Phyllis puts her arms around him in complete surrender.

NEFF: Don't tell me it's because you've
                     been in love with me all this time.

PHYLLIS: No. I never loved you, Walter. Not
                     you, or anybody else. I'm rotten to
                     the heart. I used you, just as you
                     said. That's all you ever meant to
                     me -- until a minute ago. I didn't
                     think anything like that could ever
                     happen to me.

NEFF: I'm sorry, baby. I'm not buying.

PHYLLIS: I'm not asking you to buy. Just
                     hold me close.

Neff draws her close to him. She reaches up to his face and kisses him on the lips. As she comes out of the kiss there is realization in her eyes that this is the final moment.

NEFF: Goodbye, baby.

Out of the shot the gun explodes once, twice. Phyllis quivers in his arms. Her eyes fill with tears. Her head falls limp against his shoulder. Slowly he lifts her and carries her to the davenport. He lays her down on it carefully, almost tenderly. The moonlight coming in at the French doors shines on the anklet. He looks at it for the last time and slowly turns away. As he does so, he puts his hand inside his coat and it comes out with blood on it. Only then is it apparent that Phyllis' shot actually did hit him. He looks at the blood on his fingers with a dazed expression and quickly goes out of the room, the way he came

D-21   EXT. DIETRICHSON HOME - (NIGHT)

Neff comes out of the house. He closes the front door with his right hand. His left arm hangs limp. He takes a few steps down the walk, then suddenly hears somebody approaching. He moves behind the palm tree near the walk.

A man comes up the steps towards the front door - Zachette.
Just as he reaches the door, Neff calls to him.

NEFF: Hey you. Come here a minute.
                    I said come here, Zachette.

Zachette turns and approaches him slowly.

NEFF: The name is Neff.

ZACHETTE: Yeah? And I still don't like it.
                    What do you want?

NEFF: Look, kid, I want to give you a
                    present.

He takes some loose change out of his pocket and holds out
a coin.

NEFF: Here's a nice new nickel.

ZACHETTE: What's the gag?

NEFF: Suppose you go back down the hill to
                    a drug store and make a phone call.

Neff starts to drop the nickel into Zachette's handkerchief
pocket. Zachette knocks his hand away.

ZACHETTE: Keep your nickel and buy yourself
                    an ice cream cone.

NEFF: The number is Granite 0386. Ask
                    for Miss Dietrichson. The first
                    name is Lola.

ZACHETTE: Lola? She isn't worth a nickel.
                    And if I ever talk to her, it's
                    not going to be over any telephone.

NEFF: Tough, aren't you? Take the nickel.
                    Take it and call her. She wants you
                    to.

ZACHETTE: Yeah? She doesn't want any part
                    of me.

NEFF: I know who told you that, and it's
                    not true. She's in love with you.
                    Always has been. Don't ask me why.
                    I couldn't even guess.

11-27-43   (Continued)

D-21   (Cont'd)

Zachette just stares at him. Neff moves again to put the
nickel into Zachette's pocket. This time Zachette allows
him to do it.

NEFF: Now beat it. Granite 0386, I told
                 you.

He motions toward the street below.

NEFF: That way.

Zachette goes slowly past him. Neff grabs him and pushes
him almost violently down the walk. Zachette goes out of
shot. The sound of his steps dies away as Neff looks after
him. Then, far off in the distance, the SIREN OF A POLICE
CAR is heard.

Neff moves off through the shrubbery toward the side of the
house where he parked his car.

DISSOLVE TO:

D-22   NEFF'S OFFICE - (NIGHT)

The desk lamp is still lighted. Outside the windows, the
dawn is slowly breaking.

Neff is still clutching the horn of the dictaphone. There
are eight or nine used cylinders on the desk beside him.
A widening stain of blood shows on the left shoulder of his
gray jacket. He is very weak by now, and his voice holds a
note of utter exhaustion.

NEFF: It's almost four-thirty now, Keyes.
                 It's cold. I wonder if she's still
                 lying there alone in that house, or
                 whether they've found her by now.
                 I wonder a lot of things, but they
                 don't matter any more, except I want
                 to ask you to do me a favor. I want
                 you to be the one to tell Lola, kind
                 of gently, before it breaks wide open...
                 Yes, and I'd like you to look after her
                 and that guy Zachette, so he doesn't
                 get pushed around too much. Because . . .

Suddenly he stops his dictation with an instinctive feeling
that he is not alone in the room.

As he turns in his chair the CAMERA PULLS BACK slowly. The
office door is wide open. Keyes is standing a few steps
inside it. Behind him, on the balcony outside, stands the
night watchman and the colored janitor, peering curiously
into the room over Keyes' shoulder.

11-27-43   (Continued)

SK   DOUBLE INDEMNITY   D-28
                                                                  (110)
D-22   (Cont'd)

Slowly, and without taking his eyes off Neff's face, Keyes
reaches back and pushes the door shut.

Neff hangs up the dictaphone horn. He looks at Keyes with a
faint, tired grin and speaks very slowly.

NEFF: Hello, Keyes.

Keyes moves towards him a few steps and stands without
answering.

NEFF: Up pretty early, aren't you? I always
                  wondered what time you got down to work.

Keyes, staring at him, still does not answer.

NEFF: Or did your little man pull you out of
                  bed?

KEYES: The janitor did. Seems you leaked a
                  little blood on the way in here.

NEFF: Wouldn't be surprised.

Neff makes a motion indicating the used cylinders standing
on the desk.

NEFF: I wanted to straighten out that
                  Dietrichson story for you.

KEYES: So I gather.

NEFF: How long have you been standing there?

KEYES: Long enough.

NEFF: Kind of a crazy story with a crazy
                  twist to it. One you didn't quite
                  figure out.

KEYES: You can't figure them all, Walter.

NEFF: That's right. You can't, can you?
                  And now I suppose I get the big speech,
                  the one with all the two-dollar words
                  in it. Let's have it, Keyes.

KEYES: You're all washed up, Walter.

NEFF: Thanks, Keyes. That was short anyway.

They stare at each other for a long moment, then, with intense effort Neff gets up on his feet and stands there
swaying a little. His face is covered with sweat. His
shoulder is bleeding. He is on the verge of collapse.

D-22   (Cont'd)

KEYES: Walter, I'm going to call a doctor.

NEFF: (Bitterly)
What for? So they can patch me up?
So they can nurse me along till I'm
back on my feet? So I can walk under
my own power into that gas chamber up
in San Quentin? Is that it, Keyes?

KEYES: Something like that, Walter.

NEFF: Well, I've got a different idea.
Look here. Suppose you went back
to bed and didn't find these cylinders
till tomorrow morning, when the office
opens. From then on you can play it
any way you like. Would you do that
much for me, Keyes?

KEYES: Give me one good reason.

NEFF: I need four hours to get where I'm
going.

KEYES: You're not going anywhere, Walter.

NEFF: You bet I am. I'm going across the
border.

KEYES: You haven't got a chance.

NEFF: Good enough to try for.

KEYES: You'll never make the border.

NEFF: That's what you think. Watch me.

Neff starts to move towards the door, staggering a little,
holding himself upright with great effort.

KEYES: (In a voice of stony calm)
You'll never even make the elevator.

Neff has reached the door. He twists the knob and drags
the door open. He turns in it to look back at Keyes' im-
placable face.

NEFF: So long, Keyes.

Neff goes out, leaving the door wide open. **THE CAMERA
FOLLOWS** his staggering walk along the **BALCONY TOWARDS THE
ELEVATOR LOBBY.** The sound of his breathing is so harsh

11-27-43   (Continued)

SK   <u>DOUBLE INDEMNITY</u>   D-30
(112)
D-22   (Cont'd)

and loud that for a moment it dominates the scene. Finally
he reaches the swing doors leading into the lobby and starts
to push them open. At this moment he collapses. He clutches
the edge of the door and as it swings around with him he
falls to the floor. He tries to struggle up but cannot rise.

In background comes the sound of a telephone being dialed.

KEYES'   Hello ... Send an ambulance to the
VOICE: Pacific Building on Olive Street ...
           Yeah ... It's a police job.

There is the sound of the phone being replaced in its
cradle. Then there are footsteps growing louder along the
balcony and Keyes walks slowly into the shot. He kneels
down beside Neff.

KEYES: How you doing, Walter?

Neff manages a faint smile.

NEFF: I'm fine. Only somebody moved the
          elevator a couple of miles away.

11-27-43   (Continued)

D-22   (Cont'd)

    KEYES: They're on the way.

    NEFF: (Slowly and with
                      great difficulty)
              You know why you didn't figure
              this one, Keyes? Let me tell
              you. The guy you were looking
              for was too close. He was right
              across the desk from you.

    KEYES: Closer than that, Walter.

The eyes of the two men meet in a moment of silence.

    NEFF: I love you too.

Neff fumbles for the handkerchief in Keyes' pocket, pulls
it out and clumsily wipes his face with it. The handkerchief drops from his hand. He gets a loose cigarette out
of his pocket and puts it between his lips. Then with
great difficulty he gets out a match, tries to strike it,
but is too weak. Keyes takes the match out of his hand,
strikes it for him and lights his cigarette.

FADE OUT

                              THE END

                (See following pages for alternate ending)

11-27-43

D-22   (Cont'd)

KEYES: They're on the way.

NEFF: (Slowly and with
                      great difficulty)
           You know why you didn't figure this
           one, Keyes? Let me tell you. The
           guy you were looking for was too
           close. He was right across the desk
           from you.

KEYES: Closer than that, Walter.

The eyes of the two men meet in a moment of silence.

NEFF: I love you too.

Neff fumbles for the handkerchief in Keyes' pocket, pulls
it out and clumsily wipes his face with it. Then, clutching
the handkerchief against his shoulder, he speaks to Keyes
for the last time.

NEFF: At the end of that...trolley line...
           just as I get off...you be there...
           to say goodbye...will you, Keyes?

<u>FADE OUT</u>

<u>END OF SEQUENCE "D"</u>

11-27-43

SEQUENCE "E"

FADE IN:

E-1   <u>WITNESS ROOM IN DEATH CHAMBER - SAN QUENTIN</u> (DAY)

Showing the witness room and approximately one-half of the
gas chamber. BOOM SHOT towards guard standing BACK TO
CAMERA at entrance door. Except for this guard the room
is empty.

Guard opens the door. Two other guards enter, followed by
a group of witnesses and newspaper men, each of whom removes
his hat as he enters the room. They form a group around the
outside of the gas chamber, some looking in through the
glass windows, some standing in the background on low
platforms against the wall.

THE CAMERA SLOWLY BEGINS TO MOVE IN AND DOWN, AND CENTERS
ON Keyes, as he enters the room and stands behind the door.
His face is seen through the bars of the door, which is
then closed, and CAMERA MOVES TO A CLOSEUP. His eyes
follow the action of the closing door, then slowly look
towards the gas chamber.

E-2   <u>THE GAS CHAMBER</u>, EMPTY

On its windows show reflections of the spectators, including the face of Keyes.

The door to the gas chamber opens in the background, and
beyond that another door opens. Neff comes in between two
guards. He is wearing a white open-necked shirt, blue
denim pants, and walks barefooted on a cocoanut matting. He
moves into the gas chamber, looks through the windows in the
direction of Keyes and nods quickly, recognizing him. The
guards turn him around and seat him in one of the two metal
chairs, with his back to the witnesses. They strap his
arms, legs and body to the chair. The guards go out.

E-3   <u>THE DOOR TO THE GAS CHAMBER</u>

It is open. The three guards come out of the gas chamber
into the ante-chamber, where stand the warden, executioner,
two doctors, the minister and the acid man, and possibly
several guards.

The executioner and one guard close the door. The guard
spins the big wheel which tightens it. The wheel at first
turns very quickly, then, as it tightens, the guard uses
considerable force to seal the chamber tight. The guard
steps out of the shot. The gas chamber is now sealed.

E-4   THE WITNESSES AND KEYES

They are intently watching Neff in the gas chamber.

11-27-43

E-5   THE ANTE-CHAMBER

The warden looks slowly around the room, sees that everyone is in his proper place and that the stethoscope, which one doctor holds, is connected with the outlet in the wall of the gas chamber. Also that the man in charge of the acid is ready. The warden makes a motion to the acid man. The acid man releases the mixed acid into a pipe connecting with a countersunk receptacle under Neff's chair. (This action is only suggested). The warden looks at the clock, then turns to the executioner and nods.

E-6   THE EXECUTIONER - MED. SHOT - CAMERA SHOOTING DOWN FROM HIGH ANGLE TOWARDS EXECUTIONER

He pushes a metal lever. (This immerses the pellets of cyanide in the acid under the chair.)

E-7   INT. GAS CHAMBER - MED. SHOT

CAMERA IS SHOOTING ABOVE Neff's head (just out of shot), towards spectators standing outside the gas chamber, Keyes in the center. Gas floats up into scene between CAMERA and spectators. Keyes, unable to watch, looks away.

E-8   THE FIRST DOCTOR - CLOSE SHOT

as he listens on stethoscope connected with the gas chamber. He glances at the clock above his head.

E-9   THE SECOND DOCTOR - CLOSE SHOT

He stands to right of the gas chamber door, taking notes on a pad. He glances towards First Doctor (out of scene) and looks through venetian blinds into the gas chamber. The acid man stands near him.

E-10   THE FIRST DOCTOR -

CAMERA SHOOTING FROM HIGH ANGLE TOWARDS HIM as he listens on stethoscope. The doctor glances at the clock again. He takes his stethoscope from his ears. He nods to the warden, This indicates that the man is dead. CAMERA PANS with warden as he turns to open the door connecting the ante-chamber with the witness room.

E-11   THE WITNESS ROOM - LONG SHOT FROM HIGH ON BOOM DOWN ON WITNESSES GROUPED AROUND GAS CHAMBER

The door connecting with the ante-chamber opens. A guard comes through.

GUARD: That's all, gentlemen. Vacate the chamber, please.

11-27-43   (Continued)

E-11   (Cont'd)

        The guard withdraws and closes the door by which he entered.
        The witnesses slowly start to file out. A guard has opened
        the outer door. The witnesses put their hats on as they pass
        through. A few go close to the windows of the gas chamber
        to look in at the dead man before they leave.

        All the witnesses have now left, except Keyes, who stands,
        shocked and tragic, beyond the door. The guard goes to him
        and touches his arm, indicating to him that he must leave.
        Keyes glances for the last time towards the gas chamber and
        slowly moves to go out.

E-12   CORRIDOR OUTSIDE THE DEATH CHAMBER

        CAMERA SHOOTING IN THROUGH THE OPEN DOOR AT KEYES, who is
        just turning to leave. Keyes comes slowly out into the dark,
        narrow corridor. His hat is on his head now, his overcoat is
        pulled around him loosely. He walks like an old man. He
        takes eight or ten steps, then mechanically reaches a cigar
        out of his vest pocket and puts it in his mouth. His hands,
        in the now familiar gesture, begin to pat his pockets for
        matches.

        Suddenly he stops, with a look of horror on his face. He
        stands rigid, pressing a hand against his heart. He takes
        the cigar out of his mouth and goes slowly on towards the
        door, CAMERA PANNING with him. When he has almost reached
        the door, the guard stationed there throws it wide, and a
        blaze of sunlight comes in from the prison yard outside.

        Keyes slowly walks out into the sunshine, stiffly, his head
        bent, a forlorn and lonely man.

        FADE OUT

                          THE END

Designer:	Nicole Hayward
Compositor:	Integrated Composition Systems, Inc.
Text:	10/15 Janson
Display:	Francis Gothic